Praise for Sentipensante Pedagogy

"In this highly inspiring book, Laura Rendón draws on the wisdom tradition of her Latino ancestors and her personal and courageous journey in education to offer a road map of what is possible if we are willing to embrace a vision of education that balances the inner life and ways of knowing and thinking with the outer life of just action and compassionate service to the world. She challenges us to embrace a pedagogy of wholeness that has the potential of totally transforming our schools and academies by reclaiming them as soulful places of relationship-centered learning and teaching rooted in social justice and equity. Through her moving and authentic examples of herself and others, Rendón creates promise, hope and inspiration by giving us the framework and tools to make this vision of education a reality."

—**Linda Lantieri,** Director, The Inner Resilience Program,
and author of *Building Emotional Intelligence:
Techniques for Cultivating Inner Strength in Children*

"Laura Rendón has done a beautiful thing. She has mindfully, thoughtfully, and with great clarity seen and named our familiar habits of thought, belief, and practice that limit the dynamic evolution of how we lift up, honor, and educate the precious hearts, minds, and bodies of our children.

Laura has sifted these complex threads through the lens of her fine mind and good heart, offering us a clear and colorful tapestry of guidance and companionship on a fresh, imperative educational adventure.

We cannot ever honestly claim to nourish a new generation of souls unless we ourselves are actively and vitally alive and well. Through beginner's mind, a contagious sense of wonder, and a deeply courageous vision for what is possible, she offers us the ultimate gift of education: The unlimited capacity to grow a world of human beings deeper, stronger, wiser, and more loving."

—**Wayne Muller,** founder of Bread for the Journey,
ordained minister, therapist, and author
of the national best-seller *Legacy of the Heart*

"Anyone who has yearned for a fresh vision of teaching and learning for the 21st century should read *Sentipensante*. Laura Rendón has written a book that is both deeply personal and prophetic. She balances scholarly familiarity with educational theory and history with the demographic reality that is already upon us: the changing composition of our classrooms on all measures of diversity. This is the future. Written as a manifesto to her fellow faculty and kindred administrative spirits, Laura recognizes that not all will be up for the personal and professional challenge that this remaking of the academy entails. For those who are, it offers practical advice, courage, and inspiration. Like all work at the intersection of diversity and contemplative practice, this is a book that will change lives."

—**Thomas B. Coburn,** President, Naropa University

"Reading this book is like taking a drink of cool, clear, fresh water—both refreshing and invigorating. Professor Rendón calls us to examine how higher education is and has been, and to envision how it is becoming and can be. A pedagogy that embraces wholeness, social justice, and liberation will prepare students to create and sustain a world in which social equity and justice, economic sufficiency, and a healthy planet—the triple bottom line in sustainable community building—can be achieved. And if we are to foster student success, the journey toward wholeness and authenticity must begin with we who teach, learn, lead, and serve in higher education."

—**Stephen K. Mittelstet,** President, and **V. Sue Jones,** Director, Center for Renewal & Wholeness in Higher Education, both at Richland College

"Rendón has written a pedagogic masterpiece with immense potential to transform teaching and learning in the K-12 system. Her pedagogy gives voice to what teachers have been yearning for in their hearts and minds."

—**Héctor Garza,** President, National Council for Community and Education Partnerships, Washington, DC, and Monterrey, Mexico

sentipensante

(SENSING / THINKING)

pedagogy

sentipensante
(SENSING / THINKING)
pedagogy

EDUCATING FOR WHOLENESS,
SOCIAL JUSTICE, AND LIBERATION

LAURA I. RENDÓN

Stylus
PUBLISHING, LLC.

STERLING, VIRGINIA

Published by Stylus Publishing, LLC
22883 Quicksilver Drive
Sterling, Virginia 20166-2102

Library of Congress Cataloging-in-Publication Data
Rendón, Laura I.
    Sentipensante (sensing/thinking) pedagogy : educating for wholeness, social justice
and liberation / Laura I. Rendón.
        p.   cm.
    Includes bibliographical references and index.
    ISBN 978-1-57922-325-0 (cloth : alk. paper)
    1. Education, Humanistic. 2. Holistic education. 3. Critical pedagogy.
4. Multiculturalism. 5. Education—Aims and objectives. I. Title.
LC1011.R428   2009
370.11'2—dc22

                                                    2008025793

13-digit ISBN: 978-1-57922-325-0 (cloth)

Printed in the United States of America

All first editions printed on acid free paper
that meets the American National Standards Institute
Z39-48 Standard.

Bulk Purchases

Quantity discounts are available for use in workshops
and for staff development.
Call 1-800-232-0223

First Edition, 2009

10   9   8   7   6   5   4   3   2   1

Para mis ancestros, *who intuitively knew*
the way of the heart and mind.
How long I have been waiting for you!
And to the teachers/artists/healers/activists/humanitarians
of the world—In Lak'ech
(I am you and you are me).

Contents

Contents

Foreword

I FIRST MET LAURA RENDÓN WHEN SHE SERVED AS A FETZER FELLOW FROM 1998 to 2001. So it is no surprise that her gifts and dedication as a teacher and thinking-feeling elder have become manifest in this very useful book. Laura is one of those devoted guides who opens the space between human beings with care and then enters it as well. As such, this is at once a personal and global journey. Always at the heart of this endeavor is Laura's commitment to the questions: What is the foundation and value of the classroom experience? What types of classroom inquiries and activities will be liberating and transforming?

In very real ways, this book is an invitation to make our classrooms matter. With a clear heart and a strong mind, Laura traces the divisions of being that have reduced what education can be and has reinvigorated a holism in how we question and know. She has enlisted resources from the wisdom traditions, especially from the Latino roots of spirituality. At the heart of this effort is the reunification of the mind and the heart as the living center by which we know who we are, stay connected, and care for the world we are given to steward.

In particular, the book benefits from a tireless inquiry into the dynamics of learning that have gone awry in the modern age and the reapplication of wisdom and skillful means that have worked throughout the centuries. Laura articulates a necessary rebalancing where inner knowing is as valuable as the intellectual drive, where a student-centered model reestablishes a communal authority over the cult of the expert, where collaboration and relationship unlock a greater depth of knowledge than competition, and where time is seen as a developing agent of wisdom and not as something to be raced against.

In re-imagining the student as a living root that feeds the fabric of our humanity, this book, *Sentipensante (Sensing/Thinking) Pedagogy,* liberates teachers, as well, by invoking their call as listeners, healers, humanitarians, artists, and servants. Possibilities are reawakened for everyone involved. Laura has done us all a great service by bringing the allies of the past and the best of their thinking to bear on the broken classrooms of today.

I urge you to drink from this stream and, once refreshed, to turn to whomever is near, whether student or teacher, and ask again together: How do we care for the soul of each other and the world?

—Mark Nepo
Program Officer, The Fetzer Institute

Acknowledgments

I HAVE OFTEN TOLD MY FRIENDS AND COLLEAGUES THAT THIS BOOK REPRESENTS one of the most challenging yet highly rewarding endeavors of my professional life in higher education. I wish to thank the people and organizations that helped to make this work a reality. First, I am deeply indebted to the faculty and students who agreed to be interviewed for this inquiry. Unquestionably, their stories and their experiences make this book come alive. I also express my profound gratitude to the Fetzer Institute and the Fetzer Fellows, class of 1998–2001, for supporting my work and for providing a family of spiritual warriors who touched my heart in a way it had never been touched before. I am also most appreciative of the individuals who read and reviewed some portions of this book at different times over the past several years, including Norma Cantú, Aida Hurtado, Amaury Nora, Nana Osei-Kofi, Corly Brooke, Riyad Shahjahan, Ellie Hernandez, and Armando Espinoza. I also thank two of my graduate assistants, Vijay Kanagala and Philip Vasquez, for assisting me with the conceptual and technical aspects of completing this book. And I thank my family in Laredo, Texas, for their prayers, blessings, and unending support. When all is said and done, I know I can always count on them.

Every author needs a publisher who believes in her. John von Knorring from Stylus Publishing heard me speak about this book when it was only a seed planted in my mind and in my heart. Immediately he indicated an interest in my work, and he has been ever so patient with me as I took time to develop my ideas, test them with national audiences, and finally produce what is now in your hands.

Every time I wrote, every time I took the time for deep reflection, I felt the love and guidance of my ancestors. I offer this work to them and to the universe in hopes that this ever-so-small endeavor brings educators one step closer to realizing a new pedagogical vision based on wholeness, love, and compassionate action to heal and sustain our world.

—Laura I. Rendón
Iowa State University
2008

Introduction

A NEED FOR A
NEW DREAM OF EDUCATION

*Intuition and intellect do not operate separately, but require each other's coop-
eration in almost every case. In education, to neglect the one in favor of the
other or to keep them apart cannot but cripple the minds we are trying to assist
in their growth.*

—Rudolf Arnheim, 1985

The purpose of this book is to assist in guiding the transformation of teaching
and learning in higher education so that it is unitive in nature, emphasizing the
balanced, harmonic relationship between two concepts, such as intellectualism
and intuition, teaching and learning, the learner and the learning material, and
Western and non-Western ways of knowing. I seek to shatter the belief system
that has worked against wholeness, multiculturalism, and social justice. While
the central themes foreground college and university teaching and learning, I
point out that key ideas expressed in this book—especially those related to
wholeness, multiculturalism, and contemplative practice, as well as helping students to release limiting views about themselves, fostering high expectations,
and helping students to become social change agents, among others—can also
be useful to primary and secondary school teachers.

The book is framed around a learning inquiry based on my personal journey in education and experiences as a college professor. I also draw from interviews I conducted with 15 faculty members at 2- and 4-year colleges who were

breaking new ground in working with a pedagogic model based on wholeness and consonance.

Core Question

The core question guiding my inquiry was: What is the experience of creating a teaching and learning dream (pedagogic vision) based on wholeness and consonance, respecting the harmonious rhythm between the outer experience of intellectualism and rational analysis and the inner dimension of insight, emotion, and awareness? I direct readers who seek a detailed account of how I conducted my learning inquiry to the Appendix.

Following a Different Path

Why do I write a book that dares to invoke issues of wholeness and spirituality—topics that are often considered to be highly personal or too controversial to discuss publicly in higher education? Why, as a scholar of color who has worked hard to establish herself in the academy, do I take what some would consider a perilous turn in my career to break away from some of the conventions and values of the academy I have been so well socialized to follow and deify?

I follow a different path because I believe we need a refashioned dream of education based on wholeness, consonance, social justice, and liberation. In many ways, we have lost sight of the deeper, relationship-centered essence of education, and we have lost touch with the fine balance between educating for academics and educating for life. It is time to reconnect with the original impulse that guided many of us into education—to bring our passion for teaching and learning and our minds and hearts into a profession that many educators, like me, believe is based on service to others and the well-being of our society. Many educators are disillusioned with a vision of education that is mainly focused on academic standards for learning, competitive testing and learning, grades and reports cards, the separation of teacher and learner, and the emphasis on covering only academic content. In this vision very little, if any, space is left for *inner work,* time for reflection to examine the deeper meaning of what we are teaching and what we are learning. Very little time is spent on cultivating relationships among students and between teachers and students. Precious little time is spent on helping students to work with others, deal with emotions, recognize personal strengths, develop social responsibility, be good listeners and communicators, resolve conflicts ethically and creatively, and embrace diversity as well as what we hold in common. Our present dream of education privileges intellectual development, and social, emotional, and spiritual development are viewed as tangential to academic matters. Consequently, the harmonious rhythm of teaching and learning, which involves thinking as well as feeling, is absent in many of our classrooms.

When I was a schoolgirl, I rarely had assignments that asked me to reflect on the meaning and purpose of what I was learning. No one asked me to write about what I knew best—*mi familia, mi barrio,* my life experiences and what I had learned from them. Instead, I attended classrooms with teachers who seemed so far removed from what I represented, teachers who had been socialized to not get too close to their students, to teach the basics, day in and day out, to maintain discipline and order, and to teach a content that was foreign to me. In Laredo, Texas, I attended poorly funded schools with predominantly Mexican American children. Even so, my Mexican American heritage did not exist in the curriculum in any of my classes. I was not asked to write about my culture or to read works by Latino/Latina authors.

Classroom dynamics reinforced traditional conceptions of what a model classroom should look like. Having a quiet, orderly class was seen as the hallmark of sound educational practice. Teachers who were strict disciplinarians, who silenced students, and who even oppressed them into submissive behaviors were hailed as model educators.

Attending college was not much better. During my undergraduate years, I found faculty who were even more disconnected from me than my school teachers. Most of my predominantly White college faculty had no idea who I was, what my culture was like, and what I had struggled with to even have an opportunity to enter the doors of college life. Though I lived in south Texas, my Mexican American experience was not reflected in the curriculum, though some "Hispanic" content was covered. I remember my community college English instructor teaching George Gordon Byron's (2005) eloquent poem *Don Juan* and pronouncing it, "Don Jew-an." But I dared not question her. I had been taught to be silent. The teacher was the expert. Instead, I sat quietly; maybe I was the one who was wrong. For a long time, I secretly questioned my ability to be a good student. I wondered why my classes were so often boring and meaningless and why many of my teachers were so disconnected from their students. During my undergraduate years, there were many times I felt alone and uncared for as a student. I wanted more out of my education, but I was not sure what that "more" was.

It is amazing that some of us who experienced such examples of "teaching and learning" have been able to recapture the sense of wonder for learning, to become reflective and more in tune with our true purpose in life, and to recognize the importance of not losing touch with who we are and what the real purpose of teaching and learning is about, especially in our dramatically changing world. Nonetheless, to a large extent, and with notable exceptions, much of what I experienced many years ago still exists. The negative elements of an educational system that effectively slaughters our sense of wonder and dismisses our culture, heritage, and language also kills even our students' motivation to participate in schools and colleges. From kindergarten to college, educators are struggling with reducing high attrition rates and keeping more students enrolled until they complete their education.

And there is more. When faced with problems such as hate crimes, school violence, suicidal behaviors, depression, alcohol and drug abuse, and the psychological effects of war and terrorism on our culture, educators are woefully unprepared to deal with these issues within the confines of an educational system that devalues social, emotional, and inner-life skill development. I believe students and teachers throughout our educational system need and want a redesigned model of teaching and learning, one that recaptures our sense of wonder and prizes wholeness—that is, a model that focuses on the delicate balance between our inner life of intuition, emotion, and sense of meaning and purpose, and the outer world of action and service. In short, we need a model that speaks to our humanity, compassion, and care for our self-worth and the external world we inhabit.

The Calling and the Stirring of the Soul

Over the past few years I have been involved in numerous seminars dealing with authenticity, wholeness, and spirituality in higher education. In the process, I have had some illuminating discussions with faculty and administrators. When asked to talk about their experiences in higher education, invariably many express concerns about lack of purpose and meaning in the academy. When probed, some talk about conflicts in their departments and colleges. Others bring up issues such as fragmentation, stress, overworked lives, racism, sexism, and homophobia, as well as a sense of loneliness and isolation. There is weariness, angst, and confusion in these faculty members' eyes. Often, there is a visible tension and exhaustion in their bodies. Something is killing their spirit, but they are not sure how or why. They are not even sure how to talk about these disturbing thoughts and feelings. Yet, nearly always there is a longing, a yearning to change something in their personal and work lives. That "something" often defies definition; it begs for a language of expression. It feels spiritual, whatever spiritual means to different people. It can at once feel comfortable and uncomfortable. It whispers a calling each time we struggle with the difficulties, tensions, and pain of everyday life.

I know all too well this persistent calling. For the past 20 years something had been stirring in my soul, something I could not name, something that fixated itself in the muscles of my body and the dreams of my nights. I found myself working very hard, traveling, getting grants, publishing—in short, doing everything a faculty member who wishes to make a name for herself is socialized to do. I often felt excited with the whirlwind of academic activity around me and with the multiple opportunities to engage in even more projects. But with all of my "success," I was getting sick—physically and emotionally. The constant pain in my neck and shoulders was often unbearable. I also suffered from gastrointestinal problems and had frequent headaches. I wondered whether I was really capable of giving and receiving love. I pondered whether I was being a good role model for my students. While in my early 40s, some people I had been close to died. AIDS, stomach cancer, and heart attack— all of these ailments took some of my best friends and respected colleagues in their prime. I knew something was terribly wrong, but I had no vocabulary to define what was happening to my friends and to me other than stress, lack of physical activity, and bad nutrition. Something was calling me to make some dramatic changes in my life. At times I would start to take better care of my body, join a gym, read self-help books to assist me with dealing with emotional issues, or see a therapist to help me chart a new path in my life. Yet, in all of my attempts, I found it difficult to put the bits and pieces of the problem together so that I could have a working language to articulate what I was feeling and what I needed to do to change my life.

My Calling

Then, in the late 1990s, I received a very interesting invitation from the Fetzer Institute in Kalamazoo, Michigan. The institute had a special interest in supporting research, education, and service programs to explore the relationships among body, mind, and spirit. I was invited to join a circle of educators in a seminar concerned with bringing issues of wholeness, authenticity, and spirituality into the mainstream of higher education. It was a seminar that changed my life and the way I operate in higher education. Subsequent to this meeting, I was selected to be a Fellow of the Fetzer Institute. Over the course of about 3 years, I attended nine retreats with 17 other Fellows who turned out to be some of the most phenomenal individuals I have ever met in my life. Each Fellow was engaged in an Independent Learning Quest, a personal project of his or her choosing. My project involved a two-part journey: (a) to engage in learning more about Latino spirituality in order to enhance my own spiritual practice and (b) to learn about the true essence of teaching and learning in hopes that I might be able to fashion a pedagogical model that spoke to wholeness, authenticity, and spirituality in higher education.

Through this quest, I began to more clearly articulate my calling. I was being guided to craft a newly fashioned dream/vision of education framed with Latino ancestral knowledge, to become a more reflective, socially active scholar, and to work toward taking better care of my body and spirit. During my learning quest, I was called to carefully and insightfully reflect on concepts such as interdependence, connectedness, wholeness, and harmony. I began to explore teaching and learning as complementary, not separate, processes. I learned to appreciate the importance of the balance between inner and outer learning. I learned that teaching for wholeness called for attention to the relationships among mind, body, and spirit. Ultimately, engaging the complexities of teaching and learning as they related to the harmony of the world order brought me to focus on humility, love, social action, and openness to learning. I understood from the onset that this was one highly charged, risky (if not courageous, as so many told me!) mission. But I also knew my quest held great rewards, more than I could ever imagine.

Oppositions and Connections

In essence, the calling many of us are now hearing is about how to place in balance and how to tune in with greater awareness to what Palmer (1998) calls the *inner* and *outer landscape* of teaching and learning. We are likely to be most familiar with the outer landscape, which is related to our academic work, such as publishing, speaking, writing grants, and so on, as well as our actions in the classroom: teaching, working with students, developing curricula, and such. The inner landscape is related to self—who we are, what we hold most dear, and our sense of purpose and meaning. In education the *outer* is what we do with our minds, and is usually associated with intellectualism, rationality, and objectivity. The *inner* privileges subjectivity, intuition, emotion, and personal experience. In higher education we have learned to divorce the inner from the outer. We have learned to numb our emotions and to see everything in bits and pieces disconnected from the whole.

To this day, we deify what René Descartes proclaimed nearly 300 years ago: "I think, therefore I am," perhaps the greatest theoretical statement ever made to change the way the world approached scientific inquiry. Yet African American feminist Audre Lorde (1984), in breaking from the shackles of positivism, presents an even more compelling perspective: "I feel, therefore I can be free" (p. 100). Unfortunately, what many male and female feminists, people of color, and indigenous people have viewed as important to seeking knowledge and forming truths has become secondary to dominant views that never considered what people on the margins of society believed in their hearts and minds. Moreover, feeling and thinking do not have to be perceived as incompatible. Lorde viewed them as "a choice of ways and combinations" (p. 101). The exploration of truth calls for a balance, and often a synthesis, between the inner and outer. These seemingly opposite concepts should be viewed as complementary, rather than separate and apart. Both are important; one is not better than the other.

Indigenous people and worldwide spiritual traditions have always understood that human beings are tuned to being in relationships. The notion that "I am you and you are me," which is analogous to the unity of being expressed in Buber's (1971) *I and Thou,* is also reflected in what the Maya call *In Lak'ech.* The philosophy that opposites are two sides of the same reality is also present in the Chinese notion of yin/yang, the Vietnamese belief in *am* and *duong,* the Aztec's *"Nehual te-Tehaul ne,* and the African expression *ubuntu.* Similarly, the Hindu prayerful gesture of friendship and kindness, *namaste,* acknowledges the divine in two people who greet each other, and the notion that what is spiritual and human cannot be separated.

Complexities in Defining Spirituality and Religion

As a scholar trained in the traditions of conventional research, I was taught that what we study must have an operational definition, much of it observable and measurable. Carrette and King (2005) asserted: "There is no essence or definitive meaning to terms like spirituality or religion" (p. 3). Rather, Carrette and King believe that religion and spirituality are socially constructed terms with meanings that change over time depending on social and economic interests. The authors explain, for example, that the "modern English term 'spirituality' comes from the Latin *spiritualitas* (itself from the noun *spiritus*—'the breath of life')" (p. 34). In a review of Principe's (1983) historical analysis of the term, Carrette and King said that Principe identified different phases of the use of the term, ranging from the early biblical connotation of having a moral sense of life and controlling unrestrained desires, to the present association of spirituality with the interior life of individuals. Principe locates the latter usage as beginning in 17th-century France. Influenced by such figures as Madame Guyon (1648–1717), a focus on interiority reflected the discontent with churches' "demand for a conformist piety, and against the claims of reason in matters of faith" (Bruneau, 1998, pp. 146–147).

Problems With Individualized Spirituality

Given that spirituality and religion are socially constructed concepts with contested definitions that change over time, I agree with Carrette and King (2005) that rather than trying to define the terms, we should focus on (a) identifying forms of spirituality and religion and how they evolved and (b) determining who is benefiting from different views of the terms. According to Carrette and King, today's view of spirituality with a focus on self-development and enlightenment is problematic and stems from the field of psychology, in particular from the work of William James, Gordon Allport, and Abraham Maslow. The problem is not so much focusing on the interior life of individuals but on closing off the individual from an awareness of interdependence and one's role in society. In the authors' view, today's spirituality, with a singular focus on self-development, is nothing more than another form of psychologized religion, privatized and commodified to serve modern corporate interests. When all we do is focus on our self-awareness without a concomitant emphasis on social consciousness and action, what remains is a self-serving, individual blindness to world needs.

The authors correctly note that spirituality and religion should never be isolated from the social, political, and economic world. They are concerned that spiritually has become individualized and corporatized in order to promote the values of consumerism and capitalism. When perfumes are branded with "spiritual" names such as Zen, when corporations offer workshops on spiritual practice without acknowledging that certain business dealings are creating social injustice (low wages, limited worker benefits, and exploitation of land and resources, among many other examples), and when New Age products such as crystals and incense are sold for mass consumption and are designed to calm and make individuals feel good, this, according to Carrette and King (2005), allows people to disengage from the real social justice issues of the world and makes the individual function submissively and peacefully to advance the aims of a business-oriented ideology. "Religion is rebranded as 'spirituality' in order to support the ideology of capitalism" (Carrette & King, p. 17), which is concerned with pure profits as opposed to real engagement, critical reflection, and action to address ethical and social issues. Similarly, Shahjahan (2007) calls into question the idea that an individualized form of spirituality can be liberatory and progressive.

Social Justice and Spirituality

The form of spirituality I seek to advance is connected not only to self-development, in the form of finding meaning, purpose, and wholeness in life, but also to the promotion of social justice. For me social justice involves

- having a "critical consciousness" (Freire, 1971)—an individual's ability to recognize social and economic inequities that often result in marginalization, powerlessness, violence, and exploitation, and to take action to eradicate such inequities;
- taking action to transform entrenched institutional structures to ensure that people from all social group memberships have equal access to resources and opportunities;
- acting with love and compassion to work with people who have less privilege and resources; and
- working to heal and to provide hope for all people, especially those who are victims of social and economic inequities.

I advocate a socially engaged spirituality (Carrette & King, 2005) where individuals seek to improve their being and that of the larger collective. I believe that liberation, progress, and collective advancement *cannot* be advanced when spirituality

- focuses only on self-development and personal goals to the exclusion of the collective good,
- appropriates the rites and spiritual traditions of indigenous cultures to advance the self-interests of the wealthy without regard to the fact that these cultures have been historically marginalized and devalued, or
- is grounded only on individual aims without regard to interdependence and social justice.

On the one hand, I believe that spirituality can be very personal and intimate. At the same time, I recognize that spirituality and religion are always reflecting political and social interests—witness the civil rights movement headed by Baptist minister Martin Luther King Jr.; the Dalai Lama's quest for compassion, forgiveness, and tolerance in the world; or the right-wing conservative evangelical agenda, among many others (Carrette & King, 2005). Consequently, as I reflect on the meaning of spirituality, it feels appropriate to offer a personal definition that responds to the following three questions:

How do I think of spirituality? When I think of spirit, these words come to mind: sacred, integrative, higher purpose, awe, trust, abundance, mystery, resolution of dualities, poetic, peaceful, disturbing. Being raised Catholic, I was taught Catholic doctrine and the conventions of Catholicism. I learned to fear God and other religions. Today, while I have not totally given up my Catholic upbringing, I view God as a loving, forgiving entity, and I respect diverse religions, though I may not totally agree with everything these religions espouse. Individuals can fall into different categories of religiosity and spirituality. In today's culture, one can be religious as well as spiritual, religious but not spiritual, spiritual but not religious, as well as neither religious nor spiritual.

How does spirituality feel? Spiritual moments are fraught with emotion, some joyful and some disturbing. For example, I feel joy when babies smile at me, when a loving hand is in mine, during "aha" moments of discovery, when I listen to music, and when I share a meal with my friends. I experience joy when I smile or laugh, as well as when I shed tears of release, freedom, and awakening. Spirit is present when I experience a sense of inner peace—hearing the gentle ocean waves, watching an eagle soar in the sky, putting my arms around my friends and family members, and offering comfort to loved ones. But I have learned that spirit may also shake me up, disturb my belief system, create fear and anxiety, and make me angry. Often with difficulty, I am also learning that these tension-filled spiritual moments can be learning opportunities. If I stop and reflect, if I view the moment as what was absolutely needed to occur for me to pay closer attention to and benefit from the matter at hand, then I can embrace the shadow of the event with greater ease. At the same time I understand that what happens to people is not always detached from the external causes and events that created the problem in the first place. For example, the poor are not made poor to teach them a lesson. The poor remain in their condition largely because of oppression and neglect, and it is the responsibility of socially conscious human beings to call attention to and take action against all forms of inequities.

How am I engaged in spirituality? I am now beginning to view virtually everything I do as spiritual, for I find life with all its ups and downs to be a profound spiritual experience. Writing this book has been a spiritual experience for me. So has making myself vulnerable (as well as powerful), embracing and learning from my shadows (for example, doubts, difficulties, negative aspects of self), giving of myself and my assets, practicing random acts of kindness, allowing myself to be who I am, as well as praying, meditating, and writing poetry. I also recognize that spirit is present every time I engage in social justice activities that make a difference in the lives of others (e.g., mentoring students from low-income backgrounds, providing scholarships for poor students, calling attention to the harmful effects of discrimination and oppression in the academy, etc.). I am by no means a perfect person and have made many mistakes in life. But I find that when I give of myself to others, when I focus on how my self is connected to everything I do in life, and when I engage in the work of social justice, I make progress not only in my self-development but also in the cause of eradicating social ills and advancing the collective good.

Openings: Responding to the Calling

Throughout the history of U.S. education, pedagogical methods and theories have had an impact on current teaching and learning theory and practice.

Pedagogic Theory and Practice: A Brief History

To explore openings to transform pedagogic practice, it is useful to present a bit of history regarding important educational developments. In the late-18th and early-19th century, during the Industrial Revolution, young children represented cheap labor and were employed in production factories such as cotton mills and coal mines. Opportunities for education were limited, and children were expected to work. The Fair Labor Standards Act of 1938 prohibited the employment of minors under the age of 16 in "oppressive child labor" (United States Code, 2008). The concept of universal public education made school attendance mandatory for minors in elementary and secondary schools provided mainly by local, state, and federal government. The current U.S. educational system descends from the Industrial Revolution in providing universal education to the masses. While exceptions certainly exist, K–12 education continues to resemble a factory model where information is compartmentalized and passed out as children move along an assembly line. This factory model is obsolete because it focuses on meeting standard, basic skill requirements of an agricultural-industrial world. With the factory model students cannot graduate from high school with the skills needed to "solve complex problems, analyze abstract knowledge, communicate with precision, deal with change and ambiguity, or work well with people" (Quality Education for Minorities Project, 1990, p. 47).

Fuhrmann and Grasha (1983) note that the United States has a history of college teaching and learning that spans more than 300 years. While there have been advancements in the development of learning theories, classroom models, technological tools, and assessment processes, the teacher's role has not changed dramatically even though the purposes of education have continued to evolve. Many of today's college classrooms retain some of the features of the colonial model of education that existed between 1600 and 1800, which was designed for young men from elite family backgrounds. During the colonial period, the purpose of education was to promote the Christian religion, train men for the ministry, infuse moral standards, and discipline mental faculties. A key feature of the colonial model was the defining role of the instructor as the expert who fashioned everything that took place in the classroom: course content, assignments, assessment methods, and instructional strategies. In this model, instructors (more like tutors) fed students information and resolved all debates regarding content and what constituted fact or fiction. Students became passive recipients of information, and they memorized facts. Some of the early teaching strategies included recitation, lecture, disputations, and forensics. Students were asked to recite from books and to engage in debates, or disputations, of a thesis. Public debates (forensics) began to be employed around the middle of the 18th century. Students were assessed through public examinations given by representatives of college personnel and learned citizens (Fuhrmann & Grasha).

By the 19th century, colleges and universities began to serve a wider range of students, and teaching methods, as well as the curriculum, began to change and broaden. Influenced by German universities, intellectual development and scholarly endeavors rather than memorization were emphasized, with increased use of lectures, demonstrations, and laboratory methods, though debates occurred about the relative value of lecture and recitation methods. Later, the world's attention turned to the fear of nuclear war and being left behind in the space race. Consequently, greater attention was given to science and technology. The Vietnam War made colleges and universities more sensitive to responsibility to the community and to a curriculum that had relevance, meaning, and preparation for the world of work. During this time, three theoretical views of learning emerged: humanistic, behavioral, and cognitive. The humanistic view emphasized the notion that teachers were guides and facilitators and that students could take responsibility for their own learning in an attempt to personalize and humanize learning. Behaviorists emphasized the shaping of student behavior through proper manipulation of the environment. Cognitive views were concerned with developing student skills such as problem solving and decision making (Fuhrmann & Grasha, 1983).

The Promise of Technology

With the widespread use of computers and the Internet and online networking sites such as Facebook and MySpace, a technological revolution is now in full swing. Online courses, blended courses, electronic discussion boards, iPod downloads, blogs, YouTube, wikis, and international forums such as Second Life are clearly changing the way people learn and interact. These technologies, and the ones yet to come, all point to a revolution in education that is transforming teaching and learning. One can only guess what this technological revolution will bring to schools, colleges, and universities in the next hundred years.

Openings to Create Pedagogy Based on Wholeness and Inclusiveness

The 1960s saw an influx of students from diverse ethnic/racial backgrounds attending college. The need to address these diverse students prompted some educational theorists to revise dominant teaching and learning models and approaches that were based on teaching a homogenous group of students from privileged backgrounds. During the latter part of the 20th century, scholars such as Paulo Freire, Peter McLaren, Antonia Darder, Henry Giroux, Zeus Leonardo, Michael Apple, and Christine Sleeter, among others, proposed a view of education that came to be generally identified as "critical pedagogy," which addressed issues of providing individuals with tools to engage in self-empowerment, to strengthen democracy, and to become involved in social transformation. In addition, some academics began to challenge epistemological frameworks based on modernist rational knowing, linear developmental schemes, the notion of objectivity, the divide between theory and practice, and the exclusion of the contributions of women, indigenous people, and people of color. Feminists, scholars of color, and indigenous researchers, as well as gay, lesbian, and bisexual scholars, actively challenged colonization in their disciplines, which took the form of exclusion, trivialization, marginalization, and denial (Dei, Hall, & Rosenberg, 2000; Grande, 2004; Lather, 1991; Latina Feminist Group, 2001; Osei-Kofi, Richards, & Smith, 2004; Rendón, 2000a; Tuhiwai Smith, 1999). To a large extent these scholars opened the way for conceptualizing a curriculum of inclusion that drew from multiple views of reality. Wisdom and truth could emerge from feminine and masculine ways of knowing, quantitative and qualitative research, science and spiritual traditions of the world, ancestral teachings, personal experiences, perspectives of racial/ethnic and religious minorities, as well as from the views of gay/lesbian, bisexual and transgendered people, and dreams and meditative states that unite the self with a higher and deeper wisdom (Broomfield, 1997; Rendón, 2000a).

Feminist teaching and learning theories (Belenky, Clinchy, Goldberger, & Tarule, 1986; Gilligan, 1982) appeared in the 1980s and 1990s, and were considered relational, liberatory, political, and unitive in nature. Belenky et al. (1986) presented a model of connected teaching. The model allowed for imperfect expression of knowledge in the classroom, gave students voice and confirmation, and honored subjective experience and construction of truth through consensus, not conflict. The model also focused on building relationships among faculty and students and on welcoming diversity and creating nonhierarchical learning communities. hooks (1994) presented the concept of "engaged pedagogy," where teaching and learning emphasize

- a union of mind, body, and spirit;
- the inner life of students and teachers;
- a connection between learning in the classroom and life experiences;
- the empowerment of teachers and students.

bell hooks (1994) noted how Vietnamese Buddhist monk Thich Nhat Hanh's philosophy of engaged Buddhism influenced her thinking about engaged pedagogy, because he "offered a way of thinking about pedagogy which emphasized wholeness, a union of mind, body and spirit" (p. 14). Similarly, Palmer (1998) articulated that good teaching should address three connected, critical paths that are related to the development of the whole person: intellectual, emotional, and spiritual. Yet another model of education that received attention during the late 1990s and early 2000s was *holistic education.* Miller (1997), one of the foremost interpreters of this movement, said that holistic education is "based on the premise that each person finds identity, meaning, and purpose in life through connections to the community, to the natural world, and to spiritual values such as compassion and peace" (p. 1).

Especially in the latter part of the 1990s and early 2000s, models such as integrative learning and transdisciplinary education began to receive significant attention. Integrative learning was described in at least two ways. In a position statement from the American Association of Colleges and Universities and the Carnegie Foundation for the Advancement of Teaching (2004), integrative learning was explained as reaching "across courses, over time, and between campus and community life" (p. 1). Further,

> Integrative learning comes in many varieties: connecting skills and knowledge from multiple sources and experiences; applying theory to practice in various settings; utilizing diverse and even contradictory points of view; and, understanding issues and positions contextually. Significant knowledge within individual disciplines serves as the foundation, but integrative learning goes beyond academic boundaries. Indeed, integrative experiences often occur as learners address real-world problems, unscripted and sufficiently broad to require multiple areas of knowledge and multiple modes of inquiry, offering multiple solutions and benefiting from multiple perspectives. (p. 1)

Taking a somewhat different approach, organizations such as the Fetzer Institute, Naropa University, and the California Institute for Integral Studies recognized the importance of the relationship between the curricular and cocurricular, as well as the connections among disciplines and between theory and practice. However, these organizations also emphasized integrative learning as education that addressed the whole human being—mind, body, and spirit, as well as the integration between the outer life of vocation and professional responsibility and the inner life of personal development, meaning, and purpose.

Transdisciplinary studies build on interdisciplinary, multidisciplinary, and integrative models, yet emphasize a learning approach across, between, beyond, and outside all disciplines (McGregor, 2004). To solve complex problems and to have a deeper understanding of the world, learners can draw from knowledge that cuts through disciplinary boundaries. The key emphases of transdisciplinary education include collaboration, problem solving, real-world engagement, openness to all disciplines, rigor, and tolerance (International Center for Transdisciplinary Studies and Research, 1994; McGregor, 2004).

Often omitted from discussions of teaching and learning are the traditions of education of native people, which have existed for generations. Cajete (2000) points out that there is no word for "education" in most indigenous languages. Rather, education is best described by Cajete as "coming-to-know," which entails "a journey, a process, a quest for knowledge and understanding. There is then a visionary tradition involved with these understandings that encompasses harmony, compassion, hunting, planting, technology, spirit, song, dance, color, number, cycle, balance, death, and renewal" (p. 80). Grande (2004) connected the underpinnings of critical pedagogy to possible starting points for indigenous people to rethink theory and practice. Grande posits that Red Pedagogy is based on hope: "Not the future-centered hope of the Western imagination, but rather, a hope that lives in contingency with the past—one that trusts beliefs and understandings of our ancestors as well as the power of traditional knowledge" (p. 28).

The philosophical underpinnings of critical pedagogy, feminist teaching and learning theories, holistic education, native "coming-to-know," integrative learning, transdisciplinary studies, and Red Pedagogy have created openings to conceptualize education in a different way that is

- less fragmented and more relational,
- less autocratic and more democratic,
- less passive and more active, and
- less focused on information and facts and more focused on the shared construction of meaning,

- less concerned with privileging only intellectual development and more concerned on educating the whole person,
- less tailored to a homogenous group of students and more focused on addressing issues of diversity and multiculturalism,
- less concerned with emphasis on teaching only for knowledge and more focused on searching for vocation, the highest purpose of life, and
- less concerned with emphasis on monodisciplinary approaches and individualized learning and more interested in transdisciplinarity and collaboration.

Openings to Embrace the Spiritual in Educational Institutions

There appears to be a hunger for the spiritual in today's society and in our educational institutions. From the ever-increasing numbers of books, television programs, newsletters, Web sites, Listservs, conferences, college courses, and so forth, spirituality as a topic has certainly found its way into the United States and world society.

In the past few years we have witnessed events that cut to the core of who we are as human beings, how we handle moral and ethical crises, and how education is related to the world around us. The bombing of the federal building in Oklahoma, the killing of individuals simply because they were gay or non-White, the violence at Columbine High School, terrorist threats, virus outbreaks, the Iraq War, the tsunami in Asia, Hurricane Katrina, the Virginia Tech and Northern Illinois University killings of college students, as well as the horrific events of September 11, 2001, are all emergency 911 calls for us to focus on the larger meaning of our lives, how we treat other cultures, how we deal with conflict, and how we can protect, nurture, and improve our way of life.

In a poignant *Chronicle of Higher Education* essay, Karla Jay (2001), Pace University English and women's studies professor, recounted what she learned the day of the September 11 terror. The Pace University campus in downtown Manhattan, where she taught for 27 years, is just two blocks from where the World Trade Center Towers once stood. After the terrorist attacks Karla found herself attending a workshop on how to help students cope with shock, hysteria, and anger. She realized how much she would miss her college family were she never to see them again. Suddenly, it became okay to hug her friends and students; she was no longer afraid she would be sued for sexual harassment. In class, rather than approach Mary Shelly's *Frankenstein* only from a theoretical perspective, she connected the novel to discussions about the dangers of judging people only by their appearance and scapegoating others without proof. In the process, Karla began to see her first-generation students in a new light. She became more aware of their eagerness to learn and to attend class despite the dangers of walking next to Ground Zero and in spite of their stress and exhaustion. Karla wrote: "I felt whole again, and I learned a valuable lesson: I thought I would have to hold them together; instead, they healed my soul" (Jay, 2001, p. B20). Sadly, it often takes a tragedy for us to pay attention to the other side of academics, the one that evokes a sense of wonder in the beauty and mystery of the natural world and the realization of the sacredness of our lives.

The Organization of the Book

Here in the introduction, I present the purpose of this book and the core question guiding my learning inquiry. Further, I articulate the need for a new dream of education and discuss the calling for transformation. I also discuss complexities defining spirituality and religion, and explore several paths to attain this dream. Finally, I invite others to join me in the journey to transform our work in higher education. In chapter 1, I pave the way to create a new pedagogical dream by interrogating seven entrenched agreements that govern how we approach our work in teaching and learning. In chapter 2, I introduce the faculty I interviewed for this inquiry and briefly discuss the method I employed to interview them. Chapter 3 is devoted to describing the first pedagogical position where faculty worked with an integrative, consonant pedagogy. In chapter 4, I describe the second pedagogical position where faculty employed an integrative, consonant pedagogy rooted in social justice. Chapter 5 is concerned with lessons learned from the experience of breaking away from the entrenched vision of teaching and learning, and I also address lessons learned from assessing students, as well as what students appreciated about their instructors. In chapter 6, I outline the model of Sentipensante Pedagogy, and provide guidance for instructors who wish to employ the model. Chapter 7 is concerned with the challenges, rewards, and responsibilities of embarking on creating a new vision of teaching and learning within the context of a system that resists change. The appendix outlines the methodological approach I employed in my learning inquiry.

Invitation to a Journey

From all of my personal experiences and academic undertakings I am convinced I am not alone in my path toward developing a refashioned dream of education that honors wholeness, harmony, and social justice. I know that many faculty, administrators, and students from K–12 to higher education hold similar convictions and are ready to chart a path that takes us deeper into the real work of teaching and learning. I am struck by how many times I have been told that it is very courageous of me to put these kinds of ideas in the public eye, to risk my hard-earned academic reputation to possibly be viewed as a pseudoacademic who has opted to join the ranks of New Age zealots. But my spiritual journey and my conversations with what now must be hundreds of faculty, students, administrators, and staff in higher education reveal exactly the opposite. As I stay the course, I invite others to join me in this marvelously magical, enlightening journey to transform our work in higher education.

Centuries ago, the Maya understood the tensions and twists and turns of life journeys that are fraught with excitement and danger. Chilam Balam, a Mayan priest in the Yucatan Peninsula during pre-Hispanic oral tradition, discovered the wisdom of a prayer for a Maya rite of passage that serves to guide and sustain me when I feel apprehensive and unsure about my path (1989).

You are to wander now
Entering and departing through strange villages,
Strange rooms.
You may feel you are wandering or lost,
That your gifts and items of trade
That you carry with you
Find no favor wherever you go.

Do not turn back!
Do not go back to sleep.
Something you are accomplishing.
Something the universe is assigning you.

You are to wander
Entering and departing
From strange villages . . .
Perhaps you will achieve nothing anywhere.
It may be that the things you carry with you
And your items of trade
Find no favor in any place . . .
But do not turn back, keep a firm step . . .
Something you will achieve;
Something the Lord of the Universe will assign to you. (p. 94)

Welcome to this journey to respond to our soul's calling, to fulfill perhaps the biggest assignment of our lives. In the next chapter, I pave the way toward creating a new pedagogical Dreamfield based on wholeness and consonance.

1

Prelude to a New Pedagogical Dreamfield

If we can see it is our agreements which rule our life, and we don't like the dream of life, we need to change the agreements.
—Don Miguel Ruiz, *The Four Agreements*

Don Miguel Ruiz (1997), a healer and teacher who studied indigenous teachings of the Toltec in Mexico, said that the mind dreams 24 hours a day. When the mind is awake, we dream according to the framework of what we have been taught and what we have agreed to believe. When the mind is asleep, we lack this conscious framework and the dream changes constantly. In the awakened state, we function according to society's *Dreamfield*—a collective, holographic reflection of our shared beliefs. Ruiz elaborates on the concept of human dreaming:

NOTE: Two shorter versions of this chapter appeared in 2005 in the journal *Religion and Education* and in the newsletter *Spirituality in Higher Education*, a project of the National Study of College Students' Search for Meaning and Purpose headquartered at the University of California, Los Angeles.

The dream of the planet is the collective dream of billions of smaller, personal dreams, which together created a dream of family, a dream of community, a dream of a city, a dream of country, and finally a dream of the whole humanity. The dream of the planet includes all of society's rules, its beliefs, its laws, its religions, its different cultures and ways to be, its governments, schools, social events and holidays. (p. 2)

Origins of the Agreements

Ruiz provides additional examples: For instance, when we were born we were given a name and we agreed to the name. When we were children we were given a language and we agreed to speak that language. We were given moral and cultural values. We began to have faith in these agreements passed on to us from the adults we were told to respect and to honor. We used these agreements to judge others and to judge ourselves. As long as we followed the agreements, we were rewarded. When we went against the rules we were punished, and pleasing others became a way of life, so much so that we became not who we really are, but a copy of someone else's beliefs. As we became adults we tried to rebel against some beliefs, which we began to understand made little sense or were inflicting harm. For example, some of us may have been told we were dumb, fat, or ugly. In our educational system, some social rules have created inequalities and injustices, such as belief systems that view women and people of color as lacking in leadership as well as having limited intellectual abilities. But many of us became afraid of expressing our freedom to articulate a different truth because we feared punishment for going against the prevailing belief system, even when we had no role in creating it. The dominant belief system is powerful, entrenched, validated, and constantly rewarded by the social structure that created it—so much so that when even when we begin to see that some of the agreements in the belief system are flawed and in need of change, we find it very difficult to challenge them. Ruiz (1997) notes that we need "a great deal of courage to challenge our own beliefs. Because even if we know we didn't choose all these beliefs, it is also true that we agreed to all of them. The agreement is so strong that even if we understand the concept of it not being true, we feel the blame, the guilt, and the shame that occur if we go against these rules" (p. 11).

Like Ruiz (1997), I believe that a group of people can theorize to develop a set of agreements to guide a transformational change. For instance, a core group of higher education faculty and administrators can consciously begin to hold the same thoughts that represent a newly formed vision of teaching, research, leadership, and service. A small but critical mass of individuals can create what Gladwell (2000) calls a *tipping point,* a boiling point when an idea, trend, or social behavior, like an epidemic, bursts into society and spreads like wildfire. In higher education, our shared beliefs about teaching and learning constitute the agreements that guide our present pedagogical Dreamfield. This Dreamfield is fraught with some powerful, entrenched agreements that, though shared by many, are in need of revision because they do not completely honor our humanity and our freedom to express who we are and what we represent. In the next section, I expose the privileged agreements that govern teaching and learning in higher education. In doing so, I join the many existing voices of educational transformation to contribute to the generation of a new *tipping point*—a movement that wishes to create a new dream of education. The foundation of this dream is a more harmonic, holistic vision of education that honors the whole of who we are as intellectual, compassionate, authentic human beings who value love, peace, democracy, community, diversity, and hope for humanity.

I fully understand that attempting to change entrenched agreements can be met with great resistance. Arrien (1993) stated:

> When we are too attached to something, we often lose our objectivity about it, and thus our ability to do right by it. In a state of detachment, however, we carry the capacity to deeply care from an objective place. It is important to remember that wisdom is always flexible and seldom rigid. As we increase our capacities for flexibility, we increase our ability to express our wisdom and to let go of our attachments. (p. 122)

Arrien (1993) also offers hope:

> Across many cultures, the spirits of our ancestors literally stand behind us to support us in our life dream and purpose. Native people believe that what we do in this generation will affect seven generations to come. Any-time we don't act, the effect is the same. (p. 114)

As the ancestors stand behind us, they wonder, "Oh, maybe this will be the one to bring the good, the true and the beautiful in our nature. Maybe this will be the one to break harmful family and culture patterns. Oh, maybe this will be the one" (Arrien, 1999).

Maybe we will be the ones.

Privileged Agreements Governing the Present Pedagogical Dreamfield

To create a new teaching and learning Dreamfield that is intellectual (i.e., includes high standards of academic achievement, allows students to engage in problem solving and critical thinking, engages multicultural perspectives, etc.) and spiritual (i.e., honors our humanity; instills a sense of wonder, sacredness, and humility in our college classrooms; respects and embraces alternate cultural realities; involves social change and healing; and connects faculty and students in meaningful ways) requires an examination of at least seven agreements that are firmly entrenched in the academic culture of the academy. They are

1. the agreement to privilege intellectual/rational knowing
2. the agreement of separation
3. the agreement of competition
4. the agreement of perfection
5. the agreement of monoculturalism
6. the agreement to privilege outer work
7. the agreement to avoid self-examination

The Agreement to Privilege Intellectual/Rational Knowing

> It is one of the teachings of wisdom that the merely logical mind—when it is cut off from the intrinsically higher human feelings of wonder and the sense of the sacred—inevitably becomes a plaything of the external senses, convincing us that only what is perceived with these outward-directed senses is real.
> —Jacob Needleman, *The American Soul*

The agreement to privilege particular cerebral abilities connected with intellectual/rational knowing, such as verbal, scientific, and mathematical ability, not only praises but puts on a pedestal what Gardner (1993), who developed the theory of multiple intelligences, calls *linguistic and logical-mathematical forms of intelligence,* which we typically use to measure our IQ. IQ is linked to our faith in the scientific method, leading us to prize and reward outer knowing (intellectual reasoning, rationality, and objectivity) at the expense of inner knowing (deep wisdom, wonder, sense of the sacred, intuition, and emotions). Even fields such as religion and philosophy—disciplines we think might allow the inclusion of ritual, practice, and reflection as a part of college teaching and learning—tend to keep inner learning at arm's length and usually retain an intellectual, theoretical orientation. Paying attention to our inner life, such as meditating, praying, analyzing dreams, observing rituals, and reflecting on one's purpose and the meaning of life, is often considered anti-intellectual by traditional educators who prefer a focus on outer knowing. Moreover, inner work is closely associated with spirituality, and spirituality can be an explosive, taboo topic with many definitions espoused by some fanatics and frauds invoking spirit for their own dubious purposes.

Some individuals may be pro-religion and antispirituality. Some may consider themselves spiritual but not religious. Others view spirituality in conflict with Judeo-Christian values. Even faculty and administrators who engage in inner work tend to do it without fanfare and with little support or recognition from their colleagues. Reflection and spiritual pursuits are seen by many as "soft" kinds of activities and associated with terms such as *New Age, cult,* and even *occult.* Many educators tend to dismiss group meetings and retreats focusing on the connection between inner and outer knowing as touchy-feely events where participants inevitably wind up singing, "Kumbaya." Amusing and light as these observations might appear to be, there are deep, serious fears and tensions associated with anything that smacks of spirituality. Some faculty and administrators who embrace inner knowing are often afraid to "come out of the spiritual closet" because they are not sure how they will handle the consequences of their "disobedience" to the agreement to privilege mental knowing. These faculty know full well that they may be targets of ridicule, become associated with having low standards, lose their colleagues' respect, and even be evicted from the academy itself. These perceived consequences are unfortunate and create real harm in the form of fear and anxiety about revealing who one really is and what one holds dear.

Why should we be concerned with overprivileging one form of knowing? Needleman (2003) posits that pure mental knowledge, without the corresponding education of our emotions and instinctual life, can bring no objective truth. Instead, a one-sided perspective leads us into fundamental errors about our own place in the universe and about the laws of nature itself. A number of theories point to the notion that human intelligence is multifaceted and that a unitary view of knowledge must be challenged and replaced. These are paraphrased below.

Theory of Multiple Intelligences

Gardner's (1993a) theory of multiple intelligences is predicated on seven different ways of knowing, and he describes them in practical forms in his book *Multiple Intelligences: The Theory in Practice.* The intelligences Gardner identified are

1. Linguistic—ability to use language. Poets and writers exhibit this ability in its highest form.
2. Logical-mathematical—logical, mathematical, and scientific ability. Mathematicians and scientists have this ability.
3. Spatial—ability to form a mental model of a spatial world and to function employing the model. Sailors, engineers, surgeons, sculptors, and painters have high degrees of spatial intelligence.
4. Musical—ability to compose music. The broad range of musicians, from classical to jazz, salsa, reggae, and hip-hop, as well as indigenous drummers, may be considered to have high degrees of musical intelligence.
5. Bodily-kinesthetic—ability to solve problems or fashion products using the body. Dancers, athletes, surgeons, and people who create crafts have this intelligence.
6. Interpersonal—ability to understand other people, such as what motivates them and how they work cooperatively. Salespeople, politicians, teachers, clinicians, and religious leaders have high degrees of interpersonal intelligence.
7. Intrapersonal—ability to "form an accurate, veridical model of oneself and to be able to use that model to operate effectively in life" (p. 9). People who regularly engage in forms of contemplative practice to draw

in one's own desires, fears, and capacities to regulate one's own life are likely to exhibit this kind of intelligence.

Gardner believes that linguistic and logical-mathematical forms of intelligence may get a student into college because college entrance tests, such as the SAT, prize verbal and mathematical abilities. But what receives less attention is that college academic achievement and success in life depend on all intelligences, and Gardner (1993a) stated that "all seven of the intelligences have an equal claim to priority" (p. 8).

Gardner (1999) considered four more intelligence candidates. Naturalist intelligence refers to the ability to be attuned to the environment, its flora and fauna. Environmental activists, farmers, and botanists exhibit this intelligence. Gardner cautiously discussed spiritual intelligence, as he was aware of the controversial aspects of spirituality within the scientific and academic world. He noted three distinct senses of *spiritual.* The first is a desire to know about experiences and cosmic entities that are not readily apprehended in a material sense. The second is spiritual as achieving a state of being by such means as meditation, trance states, transcendent envisioning, or being in touch with psychic, spiritual, or noetic phenomena. The third is spiritual as a type of effect on others either through a person's activities or sheer being. While noting the problematic aspects of accounting for a spiritual intelligence, Gardner found it less of an issue to speak of an existential intelligence:

> The capacity to locate oneself with respect to the furthest reaches of the cosmos—the infinite and the infinitesimal—and the related capacity to locate oneself with respect to such existential features of the human condition as the significance of life, the meaning of death, the ultimate fate of the physical and the psychological worlds, and such profound experiences as love of another person or total immersion in a work of art. (p. 60)

Gardner (1999) also questioned whether there was a moral intelligence, cautioning, "unless we can establish with some precision the relation among knowledge, actions and values, recognizing a moral intelligence harbors significant risk" (p. 67).

Along with intellectual pursuits, we need an education that is broadly defined and that addresses the notion that we are multifaceted human beings.

Our education should assist us to develop not only our intellectual capacities, but our ability to be creative and reflective, as well as to work with and understand other people. Arrien (1993) stated:

> As we move into the twenty-first century, it is the work of all human beings to attend to the health of both our "inner" and "outer" houses: the inner house of our selves, the limitless world within; and the outer house of the world in which we live our daily lives. Many people in contemporary society feel little or no connection between these two worlds, a state that indigenous, land-based people of the earth, whose cultures reach back thousands of years, would find not only sad but incomprehensible. (p. 3)

Education should help us turn inward as we learn to appreciate who we are and develop a philosophical orientation to engage in life work.

Emotional Intelligence (EQ)

Goleman (1995) referred to emotional intelligence as EQ, and discusses its connection to neural systems in the brain linked to cognitive skills and knowledge. According to Goleman (1998), "Our emotional intelligence determines our potential for learning the practical skills that are based on its five elements: self-awareness, motivation, self-regulation, empathy, and adeptness in relationships" (p. 24). Goleman noted that EQ is far more important than IQ for job performance and leadership. It is also important to note that brain researchers are making an important link between cognition and emotion. Damasio (1994) and Greenspan (1997) give neuroscientific research findings showing that reason and emotion are not separate and irreconcilable. In fact, the absence of emotion can impair rationality, making wise decision making almost impossible. Drawing from an extensive review of research in psychology and anthropology, as well as from the writings of philosophers, writers, and musicians, Nussbaum (2001) asserts that emotions form a part of our system of ethical reasoning. Brain research is also informing how we manage ourselves and how we handle relationships. Goleman (2003) pointed to scientific experiments conducted by Richard Davidson and Jon Kabat-Zinn that document the benefits of mindfulness training in which the meditator views passing thoughts as an impartial and nonjudgmental observer. Meditation was found to affect brain activity in the left prefrontal cortex, which is associated with positive moods, such as being enthusiastic and energized, and low levels of anxiety.

Spiritual Intelligence (SQ)

Zohar and Marshall (2000) review scientific evidence carried out by neuropsychologist Michael Persinger and neurologist V. S. Ramachandran and his team at the University of California that there is a spiritual intelligence located among neural connections in the temporal lobes of the brain. This "God spot" allows the brain to ask profound questions of meaning and value. Zohar and Marshall also review the research of Austrian neurologist Wolf Singer that shows there is a neural process in the brain that gives meaning to our experience. As further evidence for the basis of SQ, Zohar and Marshall discussed the work of neurologist and biological anthropologist Terrance Deacon on language as a meaning-centered activity that coevolved with development in the brain's frontal lobes and indicated that "Deacon's whole research programme for the evolution of symbolic imagination and its consequent role in the brain and social evolution underpins the intelligence faculty we are calling SQ" (p. 13).

To paraphrase Zohar and Marshall (2000), a highly developed SQ includes the following characteristics: flexibility, self-awareness, capacity to face and use suffering, capacity to face and transcend pain, capacity to be inspired, reluctance to harm others, ability to see connections among what appears to be different, tendency to ask why or what if, field independence, and ability to work against conventional thought. Similarly, Wolman (2001) defines the characteristics of spiritual intelligence. Wolman developed the PsychoMatrix Spirituality Inventory (PSI). After carefully studying the responses of more than 6,000 men and women, Wolman identified seven factors that make up human spiritual experience and behavior: Divinity, Mindfulness, Intellectuality, Community, Extrasensory Perception, Childhood Spirituality, and Trauma.

Heart Intelligence (HQ)

Recent research, though controversial and not thoroughly conclusive, is pointing to the notion that our hearts are also sites for intelligence. For example, studies being conducted through the Institute of HeartMath Research Center in California are attempting to provide a scientific basis to explain how the heart affects mental clarity, creativity, emotional balance, and personal effectiveness (2004). Research points to the heart's having a self-organized processing center that communicates with and influences the cranial brain in four major ways: "*neurologically* (through the transmission of nerve impulses), *biochemically* (via hormones and neurotransmitters), *biophysically* (through pressure waves) and *energetically* (through electromagnetic field interactions). Communication along all these conduits significantly affects the brain's activity."

Pearsall (1998), a psychoneuroimmunologist, employs theories and research of scientists contributing to the field of energy cardiology and cardioenergetics to explain how cells make memories out of infoenergy that is circulated through the body by the heart. Pearsall also relies on personal experience, lessons from indigenous people, and stories of heart transplant patients to make his case that the heart has intelligence. Pearsall's stories from heart transplant patients are nothing short of fascinating, demonstrating that the heart thinks, remembers, communicates with other hearts, helps regulate immunity, and contains stored information that continuously pulses through our bodies. A little girl who receives a heart transplant from a murdered child starts screaming at night. In her dreams, she recognizes the man who murdered her donor. A young man from a Spanish-speaking family begins using the word *copacetic,* which he never used before. The wife of his heart's donor says that every time she and her husband argued and made up, they would both say everything was copacetic (Pearsall, 1998, pp. 7–8, 76). Clearly, future research holds much promise to guide our society into recognizing that there is indeed more than one form of intelligence, and that life depends on multiple intelligences. If these assumptions are correct, then we are doing students a disservice by focusing primarily on linguistic and logical mathematical forms of intelligence.

We need to reframe the agreement that educational achievement and success in life depend solely on linguistic and logical-mathematical abilities.

Example of a newly constructed agreement: *agreement to work with diverse ways of knowing in the classroom.*

The Agreement of Separation

We are here to awaken from the illusion of our separateness.

—Thich Nhat Hanh

In today's educational systems, K–12 to higher education, separatism manifests itself when educational departments operate in silos, keeping the different domains of knowledge and disciplines separate with little to no collaboration between faculty who represent diverse disciplines and students who are exposed to the perspectives of only one discipline. Even within the same department, collaborative efforts among faculty are often minimal. If we agree that today's students need to be educated to live and prosper in a dynamic, ever-changing world, then we need a framework for learning that is transdisciplinary in nature, one that explores the interconnections among different disciplines in an attempt to understand and solve world problems (American Association of Colleges and Universities, 2007; Derry & Fischer, 2005). According to McGregor (2004) the hallmark of transdisciplinarity is "to obtain a deeper understanding of the world" (p. 5). To do so, a transdisciplinary approach "traverses all possible disciplines" (p. 2).

Within the classroom environment, the underlying tenets of the agreement of separation are (a) teaching and learning are linear, and information flows primarily from teacher to student; (b) faculty should keep a distance between themselves and their students; (c) faculty are the sole experts in the classroom; (d) teaching is separated from learning; (e) any kind of faculty outreach to students, such as validation, caring, or encouragement, is more often than not considered a form of coddling students who are presumed to be adults and should be strong enough to survive a collegiate environment on their own; (f) the student studies the subject matter from a distance; and (g) the student learns to understand and solve problems employing the perspectives of only one discipline.

Freire (1971) has critiqued the separatist Dreamfield of teaching and learning, calling it the "banking model of education," where faculty distance themselves from students and "deposit" their knowledge in the classroom. Freire and other critical educators, such as Peter McLaren, Antonia Darder, and Henry Giroux, argue that the banking model of teaching and learning is oppressive in nature, exploiting and dominating students, as well as working against demo-cratic structures that honor diverse voices, ways of knowing, and participation in knowledge production. Freire asks educators to transform oppressive struc-tures and to create liberatory pedagogy where teaching and learning can be democratic, participatory, and relational, allowing teachers and students to be holders and beneficiaries of knowledge. Similarly, feminist scholars (e.g., Belenky et al., 1986; Gilligan, 1977; hooks, 1994; Hurtado, 1996) have argued that a connected, holistic model of education can be liberatory in nature. Belenky et al. (1986) described a "connected teaching"approach that provides a space for student development, allows the expression of uncertainty, fosters community, honors diversity of perspectives, and views teaching as simultane-ously objective and personal.

In vogue over the past 10 years, the notion that learning is more important than teaching has given rise to "learner-centered" approaches to education. The belief is that the focus in the classroom should be on learners and learning, and not so much on teachers and teaching. While it is understandable that educa-tors would want to create a pedagogic model that works against the tendency of some teachers to be autocratic and oppressive, the key to good teaching and learning is likely found in both teachers and students. Along these lines, Palmer (1998) argued that the debate between determining whether learning is more important than teaching is premised on a false dichotomy:

> As the debate swings between the teacher-centered model, with its con-cern for rigor, and the student-centered model, with its concern for active learning, some of us are torn between the poles. We find insights and excesses in both approaches, and neither seems adequate to the task. The problem, of course, is that we are caught in yet another either-or. Whip-lashed, with no way to hold the tension, we fail to find a synthesis that might embrace the best of both. (p. 116)

Another way of keeping faculty separated from students is to avoid assist-ing students even when they need support, encouragement, and validation. When I speak with faculty about the importance of validation (Rendón, 1994), such as actively reaching out to support students and to communicate that stu-dents can learn and become a part of the college learning community, I am asked whether this is a form of coddling students. It is as if anything faculty do to assist students to succeed and to believe in themselves is a form of making students weaker. The assumption is that students, regardless of background, should "tough it out," and that all students should learn how to succeed without any intervention. While it is true that many students believe that they work best alone and are able to care for themselves, my own research (Rendón, 1994, 2002) documents that a large class of students benefit from what I call validation, "an enabling, confirming and supportive process initiated by in- and out-of-class agents that fosters academic and interpersonal development" (Rendón, 1994, p. 44). Validation theory calls for faculty and staff to get closer to students, to reach out to students to offer assistance, and to help students make social and emotional adjustments in college, if not in their personal lives. The concept of validation is similar to the notion of caring as advanced by Noddings (1984) and Valenzuela (1999) when addressing the essence of teacher/student relationships in the K–12 system. Noddings and Valenzuela note that instead of being concerned with students' subjective realities and working with a moral ethic of caring that fosters positive relationships between teachers and students, many schools are focused on detachment, impersonal and objective language, and nonpersonal content. This results in many students feeling that who they are and what they represent are not valued in school.

A separatist view of teaching and learning also works to detach the student from what is being learned. Whatever learning takes place has little to do with the learner; the learning is "out there," independent of the student. There is a significant difference between what Abraham Maslow (1988) critiqued as *spectator knowledge* and what Owen Barfield termed *participatory epistemology*. For Maslow, spectator knowledge alienated the knower from what is to be known and perpetuated a dualistic consciousness. Maslow wrote:

> What does the orthodox scientist mean by "knowing?" Let us remember that at the beginning of science the word "knowing" meant "knowing of the external physical world," and for the orthodox scientist it still does. It means looking at something that is not you, not human, not personal, something independent of you the perceiver. (p. 81)

Maslow was critiquing the notion of dualism, which is held in mass consciousness and creates a division between the knower and the known.

Finally, it is important that if students are to be educated for a rapidly changing world, they need more than in-depth knowledge in one particular discipline. Rather than a monodisciplinary approach that brings only one discipline to bear on a particular problem, students need knowledge that cuts across disciplinary boundaries (McGregor, 2004). I agree with Derry and Fischer (2005) that transdisciplinary competencies are needed to prepare students to live and work in a world that "relies on collaboration, creativity, definition and framing of problems [and requires] dealing with uncertainty, change and intelligence that is distributed across cultures, disciplines and tools" (p. 3).

We need to change the agreement that good teaching and learning evolve from a model that distances teachers from students, separates teaching from learning, alienates students from what is to be learned, and is focused on noncollaborative monodisciplinarity.
    Example of newly constructed agreement: *the agreement to embrace connectedness, collaboration, and transdisciplinarity.*

The Agreement of Competition

If you look deeply into any living being, a mosaic of intimate interrelationships will be revealed. Life is all about relationships.
        —Joel Levey and Michelle Levey, *Living in Balance*

As a society we have tended to emphasize competition far more than cooperation to explain important concepts such as educational achievement and the evolution of life itself. The philosophy of competition pits students against each other in a fiercely competitive teaching and learning environment. While abundant examples of the forces of competition can be found in nature and society (e.g., sports events, business markets, survival of life forms, etc.), what is being argued here is that focusing solely on competition does not take into account the notion that relationships and cooperation also play a central role in the survival of life forms and the intellectual and social development of individuals. The delicate balance between competition and cooperation is often unnoticed. Individual athletes depend on the team. We are individuals, yet we are also members of the earth's family. As a concept, competition has a scientific origin—Charles Darwin's natural selection theory, a form of survival of the fittest. In higher education, we know this agreement as *merit,* where only the best and the brightest, as defined by individually attained grades and test scores, are deemed worthy of attending college while others are weeded out.

But how complete is Darwin's theory? Margulis (1981), a professor of geosciences, challenged Darwin with her own theory of endosymbiosis, and argued that coming together, not competing, is what advances evolution. In short, Margulis proposed that cooperation, interaction, and mutual dependence among life forms were the driving forces behind evolution. Examples of symbiotic relationships abound in nature and in the human body itself. Marine biologists have observed numerous instances of relationships between two species. The boxer crab carries a pair of small anemones in its claws. When approached by a predator, the crab waves its claws with its stinging tentacles to deter the invader. Exemplifying the delicate balance between competing for food and surviving in the relationship, the anemones benefit from small particles of food dropped by the crab during feeding (Abbot, 2000). Botanists understand that every time human beings breathe, they depend on oxygen produced by plants. In turn, plants depend on carbon dioxide produced by the animal kingdom. Microbiologists and immunologists know that the human body is inhabited by microbes, which for the most part live in a mutually beneficial relationship. Among other things, they help humans digest food and protect against invading viruses.

Margulis's (1981) theory is truly fascinating. Not only does the theory challenge the notion that only competition matters, it offers a viable, alternative explanation for the evolution of life. Endosymbiosis is a process where cells learn to live together not by destroying each other so that the strongest survive but by merging with each other in a mutually beneficial relationship, or symbiosis. Margulis noted that it is microbes, living beings too small to be seen without the aid of advanced microscopes (which Darwin did not have), that provide the mysterious creative force in the origin of the species, and that evolution of life cannot be fully explained if microbes are omitted from the story. While society has yet to fully accept differing views of evolution and to break down the assumptions behind individualism, it is time to examine what symbiotic relationships have to add to the way students are assessed and how they are socialized in classroom environments. In other words, can we base student learning and achievement on an ontology rooted not only in individualism but also in relationships?

Perhaps only slightly in jest, Margulis (1981) explains: "Charles Darwin (1809–1882), in the absence of evidence, invented "pangenes" as the source of new inherited variation. If he and the first evolutionist, the Frenchman Jean Baptiste de Lamarck, only knew about the subvisible world that we know today, they would have chuckled, and agreed with each other and with us" (Margulis, 2002). While initially mocked by other scientists as sheer fantasy, Margulis's theory, explained in her book, *Symbiosis in Cell Evolution,* is now mainstream and considered one of the greatest achievements in evolutionary biology. The Endosymbiotic Theory of Eukaryote Evolution (Symbiotic Theory) provides an explanation for the evolution of multicelled organisms known as eukaryotes from ancestral forms of prokaryotes. In essence, the theory states that eukaryotes evolved not by random genetic mutation as previously believed, but by a number of cell combinations. The simpler, less complex prokaryotic derivatives combined or merged into a single host cell to the extent of being an inseparable structure and formed today's multicolor prokaryotes. The evolution of prokaryotes is the key to the existence and evolution of every multicellular organism in the world today. Margulis and Sagan (1986) theorize that networking, not competitive combat, is what advances life. It is not surprising that this theory is considered to explain the single most important event of the organic world: the evolution of multicelled organisms (Bond, 1996).

If Margulis's (1981) theory holds true, then what does this have to say about our work as educators? The testing mania that has hit our entire educational system, from kindergarten through graduate school, is predicated on competition that sorts high-scoring students from those who are presumed to have limited intelligence even when the tests may be culturally biased, work against students with learning disabilities, and/or measure only certain forms of intelligence, primarily verbal and logical-mathematical. In higher education, SAT and GRE scores are widely employed to rank colleges and universities that seek to gain prestige in the academic marketplace. Many students are terrified of taking these tests and decide to not even apply to college for fear they will fail and face humiliation. Some students who have attended resource-poor schools and who grow up without the advantages of affluent students usually do not do well on standardized tests. It takes a great deal of time for admissions officers to review students holistically (though some colleges and universities have taken this step). Sacks (2000) noted that a key problem with standardized mental tests is that they have limited predictive ability. For example, to get into graduate school, students are usually asked to take the GRE, but "the GRE quantitative test accounts for no more than four percent of the variation in student engineers' classroom performance" (Sacks, p. 15). As Gardner (1993) maintains, we should "spend less time ranking people and more time trying to help them" (p. 12).

While competition can certainly be a strategy that faculty may employ in the classroom, assisting students to learn can also involve creating a relationship between teachers and students. The connective aspects of teaching and learning can be lost if the classroom context is based only on competition. Learning communities, which involve a great deal of peer interaction and relationship building, have documented promising outcomes, such as increased rates of retention, high grades, as well as social, emotional, and spiritual development (Burgis, 2000; Burgis & Rendón, 2006; Cabrera, Crissman, Bernal, Nora, & Pascarella, 2002; Goodsell-Love, 1999). Learning communities have been instituted in 2- and 4-year colleges and universities. They typically involve classes that are linked or clustered during an academic term, usually with an interdisciplinary theme. A common cohort of students is enrolled, and a key strength is that the community helps to build a sense of group identity, cohesion, and specialness (Goodsell-Love, 1999). Learning communities are known to foster student engagement through collaborative learning as well as community- and problem-based learning. Students are taught to see connections among the courses they take, and community is a key condition for learning (Lardner, 2005).

We need to change the agreement that competition is the primary and most useful method to advance learning.

Example of newly constructed agreement: *the agreement to engage diverse learning strategies (i.e., competitive and collaborative learning and individual-based and community-based learning) in the classroom.*

The Agreement of Perfection

The greatest peril of the path for those who seek Enlightenment is not leaving enough room inside themselves for what they do not know. And the greatest

peril of the path for those who already are enlightened is neglecting to leave
enough room inside themselves for what they do not know.
—Andrew Cohen, *Embracing Heaven and Earth*

The agreement of perfection is witnessed in an academic model where there is usually little, if any, room for error, unknowing, and imperfection in the classroom. However, feminist learning theorists have shown that in a context where human imperfection is downplayed, many students become intimidated by professors who either bombard them with too much information or leave them confused and frustrated with too little information (Belenky et al., 1986; Gilligan, 1977). In fact, Belenky et al. assert: "In a connected class, no one apologizes for uncertainty. It is assumed that evolving thought will be tentative" (p. 221). Along the same lines, Cohen (2000) indicates that behaving as if we already know everything is a symptom of arrogance, a way that the ego protects itself from what it does not know. Moreover, overconfidence can be limiting, while being in a state of not knowing has no limitations. Cohen maintains that true learning results from a deep and continuous surrender to the unknown.

How often are we, as faculty and students, called to be perfect, to present ourselves as all-knowing experts? How often we are called to view education simply as acquiring information and not as a humble process of coming to know, of liberating our imaginations to embrace all that is sacred in the world? How often do we act as knowers instead of seekers? Cohen (2000) maintains that Enlightenment is a delicate business, involving a paradox between knowing and not knowing. He stated:

> Unless we hit the bull's eye—which means that perfect middle space between knowing and not knowing—the inevitable result of profound spiritual experiences, including even Enlightenment itself, will be imperfect. That simply means that in the one who is enlightened, a shadow of ego will remain in his or her attainment; knowing will be more powerful than not knowing. That is why the pursuit of Enlightenment is such a delicate matter for the seeker and finder—it is so easy to err on one side or the other. (p. 86)

Not only are we judged as arrogant when we behave as if we know everything, but our sense of wonder, which requires that we embrace the mystery of darkness, is also diminished. Learning, according to anthropologist Joan Halifax (1994), is not being in a state of all-knowing perfection; it is more a process of initiation, of leaving some sense of security behind us and venturing forth into the unknown. Halifax says that in our culture the word *education* means to be led out of ignorance into knowing more, and that knowledge is usually defined as the accumulation of facts and data. However, in some tribal cultures, education is not the outward experience of being led out of ignorance. Instead, the experience is an inward journey, an initiation that takes the initiate into the unknown and that is grounded in not knowing. College and university faculty need to better understand the delicate balance between knowing and coming to know. As Shunryu Suzuki Roshi eloquently expressed: "If your mind is empty, it is always ready for anything; it is open to everything. In the beginner's mind there are many possibilities; in the expert's mind there are few" (as cited in Mitchell, 1998, p. 4).

We need to revise the agreement that being in a state of tentativeness and imperfection is always a sign of intellectual weakness.

Example of newly constructed agreement: *the agreement to be open and flexible about being grounded in knowing and not knowing.*

The Agreement of Monoculturalism

> *Diversity as a way of thought and a way of life is what is needed to go beyond the impoverished monocultures of the mind.*
> —Vandana Shiva, *Monocultures of the Mind*

The agreement of monoculturalism has created an epistemological dream underscored by (a) the almost exclusive validation of Western structures of knowledge, (b) the subjugation of knowledge created by indigenous people and people of color, (c) course offerings that preserve the superiority of Western civilization, and (d) the dominant presence of faculty and administrators in colleges and universities who subscribe to monocultural paradigms of knowledge production and comprehension. Hurtado (1996) noted:

> Because of the emphasis in this country on a monocultural social and personal identity (although it really has never existed in the United States)

and the philosophical and political underpinnings of rugged individual-ism, the very notion of multiplicity has been conceptualized as deviant or pathological. (p. 375)

Modern Western science, with all of its acumen, has been critiqued on a number of fronts by some feminist researchers as well as scholars of color and indigenous scholars. One area of contestation is the erroneous assumption that Western science contains the history of all science (Broomfield, 1997; Harding, 1992; Tuhiwai Smith, 1999). Inherent in this assumption is the belief that "con-ceptions of scientific rationality, objectivity, and progress developed precisely to *distinguish* 'civilized' Europeans from 'primitive' Africans and other 'lower peo-ples' (Harding, 1992, p. 232). Despite claims that the academy is open to diver-sity and multiculturalism, the fact is that most of what gets taught and how it gets taught is predicated on a paradigmatic status quo based on what Guerrero (1996) identifies as "Euro-American privilege and the presumed superiority of West-ern civilization" (p. 49). Non-Western views of truth as espoused by third world perspectives, as well as indigenous knowledge, are at best objectified as *the other* and, at worst, as primitive and anti-intellectual. Tuhiwai Smith (1999) explained that indigenous people have often been viewed as incapable of using their minds or intellects. She wrote:

> We could not invent things, we could not create institutions or history, we could not imagine, we could not produce anything of value, we did not know how to use land and other resources from the natural world, we did not practice the "arts" of civilization. By lacking such virtues, we disqual-ified ourselves, not just from civilization but also from humanity itself. In other words we were not "fully human"; some of us were not even consid-ered partially human. (p. 25)

Vandana Shiva (1993), an internationally recognized Indian environmental-ist and feminist, emphasizes that "monocultures of the mind" manifest themselves in the preferential treatment of one class (affluent), one race (White), and one gen-der (male). In her view these monocultures pose a threat to diversity in nature and in our society, leading to a disappearance of alternatives. Shiva elaborated:

> How often in contemporary times has the total uprooting of nature, tech-nology, communities and entire civilizations been justified on the grounds

that there is no alternative? Alternatives exist, but they are denied or excluded. Their inclusion simply requires a context of diversity. Shifting to diversity as a mode of thought, a context of action, allows multiple choices to emerge. Diversity enriches our world. Monocultures impoverish it. Diversity offers a survival option. Monocultures threaten life in all its richness. (p. 2)

In higher education a monocultural framework is exhibited in curricula that exclude the contributions that women, indigenous people, and ethnic/racial minorities have made in history, art, math, science, philosophy, and literature, among other fields. Arredondo, Hurtado, Klahn, Najera-Ramírez, and Zavella (2003), Chicana feminist colleagues, highlighted the exclusion and marginalization of Chicana scholars in their book, *Chicana Feminisms.* Refusing to be silenced, Chicana scholars claim "a "third space" to resist and reject colonial ideology and to capture the complexity of Chicanas' experiences with multiple epistemologies and methods. The minimal presence and often total absence of tenured faculty of color in diverse disciplines, as well as the small number of administrators of color in high-level positions of authority, such as college president, provost, vice president, dean, or department chair, serve to control and validate Western structures of what constitutes knowledge, how knowledge gets taught, who should be hired to transmit knowledge, and what gets rewarded as exemplary teaching, research, and service. Collins (2000) elaborated on this point:

Two political criteria influence knowledge validation processes. First, knowledge claims are evaluated by a group of experts whose members bring with them a host of sedimented experiences that reflect their group location in intersecting oppressions of race, gender, class, sexuality and nation. In the United States, this means that a scholar making a knowledge claim typically must convince a scholarly community controlled by elitist, White, avowedly heterosexual men holding U.S. citizenship that a given claim is justified. Second, each community of experts must maintain its credibility as defined by the larger population in which it is situated and from which it draws its basic, taken-for-granted knowledge. This means that scholarly communities that challenge basic beliefs held in the U.S. culture at large will be deemed less credible than those that support popular ideas. (p. 253)

A one-sided monocultural framework defies the reality of multiculturalism. Higher education is admitting perhaps the most diverse student body ever, reflecting the increasing colorization of the nation. The national profile of race and ethnicity derived from the U.S. Census Bureau (2008) reveals that in 2008 non-Hispanic Whites remained the majority, making up about 66% of the U.S. population. Conversely, Hispanics were about 15.1%, African Americans 13.5%, Asians 5%, American Indians, 1.5%, and Native Hawaiians, .3%. Adding to the complexities of social constructions of race and ethnicity is the fact that by 2050 about 21% of Americans are expected to claim mixed ancestry—biracial or multiracial. Within the next 10 years a fast-growing generation of diverse students will have an impact on American college campuses, revealing a complex, multifaceted student cohort that often defies categorization (El Nasser & Overberg, 2001; Rendón, García, & Person, 2004). Adding to this complex scenario is religious diversity. Eck (2001) notes that Americans are the most religiously diverse people in the world, and our schools and colleges are attended by varieties of people from every part of the world. Of course, college and university students are also diverse in terms of gender, sexual orientation, worldview, and class. Consequently, a multiplicity of perspectives are consistently engaged (overtly and covertly) in higher education classrooms whether professors want to recognize that or not.

To push and expand theoretical paradigms regarding knowledge construction, production, and use requires a multiperspectival approach that embraces diverse ways of knowing which emerge from multiple perspectives. We need to change the agreement that Western ways of knowing are superior to all other forms of knowledge.

Example of newly constructed agreement: *the agreement of multiculturalism and respect for diverse cultures.*

The Agreement to Privilege Outer Work

Whether they are Hispanic or Native American, Caucasian or Black, the more their lives speed up, the more they feel hurt, frightened, and isolated. Despite their good hearts and equally good intentions, their work in the world rarely feels light, pleasant, or healing. Instead, as it all piles endlessly upon itself, the whole experience of being alive begins to melt into one enormous obligation. It becomes the standard greeting everywhere: I am so busy.

—Wayne Muller, *Sabbath*

I was turning 50 when one of my friends and colleagues, a 44-year-old professor, was diagnosed with colon cancer. We had not seen each other in a while,
and when I heard about her diagnosis I sent her an e-mail and asked if I could
come visit her. I went to her home where we had time to catch up with each
other for about two hours. She told me she had gone through "a wake-up call,"
but she was hoping for the best. Only a few weeks later, I went to see her again
at the hospital, this time with a group of junior scholars. Her condition had gotten much worse. What I remember most about what she told us was that at this
particular stage of her life, writing the next article or the next book was not what
counted. The two most important things she longed for were to be able to sleep
and eat normally. I remember that one by one, we all said what were to be our
last good-byes. As I exited her room, I saw the young scholars outside hugging
each other, full of emotion. I realized that our tears were not just for the friend
we were losing. Our grief was also for us, for having just painfully and abruptly
experienced our own wake-up call to slow down, assess the error of our ways,
and recognize that there is more to life than our academic work.

The struggle for balance in my personal and academic endeavors, to accept
invitations only when I can be fully present, and to say no when I really need
more time for myself and my loved ones is ever present in my life. In a world
where outer work seems to be important, I find that I must be flexible and focus
on keeping my priorities in order. In my 30s and 40s, I was literally running on
adrenaline. I worked long hours and weekends, accepted projects without
reflecting on the impact they might have on my academic and personal life,
traveled extensively, and thrived on being on an "academic high." I rationalized
that this workaholic lifestyle was worth it because my work was about making
a difference for students who, like me, grew up in poverty and wanted a better
life for themselves. The problem was that I forgot about making a difference
for me. The memory of daily headaches, neck and shoulder pain, gastrointestinal problems, and sheer exhaustion is still fresh in my mind. My workaholic style gave me the highs of achievement and the lows of exhaustion. Sure,
I accomplished a great deal and earned promotion and tenure. But my personal
life suffered for it. I found it difficult to give and to receive love, and there were
many times when I felt lonely and isolated, even with multiple activities and
with many people around me. Around middle age, I experienced my own

epiphany, a time when I began to feel that enough was enough, that I did not want to die young, that I deserved to have love in my life, and that I could still do good work and work hard without losing myself in the process. Fortunately, through a great deal of inner work by myself and in community with others, I have grown over the past 5 years to the point that I am finding it easier to walk my talk, but not without difficulty. Like any drug, alcohol, or food abuser, it is easy to fall back into destructive patterns even when one tries to change negative behaviors.

My life and the lives of so many others who work in the academy provide ample examples of the agreement to privilege outer work, to concentrate on keeping ourselves constantly busy with multiple projects often to the point of burnout, stress, and illness. Faculty and administrators are socialized to believe that the best academics are those who are constantly publishing, getting millions of dollars in grants, putting in long hours, working on weekends, and traveling extensively. When we ask our colleagues: "How are you?" we almost never get the answer: "Oh, I am so relaxed! I got so much rest this weekend. I had time to do everything I wanted to do with my family." In one of my many trips, I was reading the airline's magazine, and I was struck by an article reporting that Americans receive an average of 28 days of vacation a year, while Europeans receive 47. Nonetheless, employees in America are leaving $21 billion worth of unused vacation days on the table at the end of the year. Some of the reasons cited for not taking vacations were too much work to do, fear of being labeled obsolete if away from the office too long, and guilt about leaving coworkers in a lurch. Muller (1999) maintains that lack of rest, poor nutrition, and lack of exercise is a form of bodily violence often resulting in disease, poor relationships with our loved ones, constant stress, burnout, drug and alcohol abuse, and even death. In a study involving close to 200 faculty members, Astin and Astin (1999) found that faculty experienced a wide range of negative reactions to stress, including "health problems, divorce, over consumption of caffeine and sleep deprivation" (p. 27). While working hard to make more money has its merits, Nepo (2000) noted that love, truth, and compassion are what matter most in life, and that money is best used "to make love work, to bring truth into being, to allow generosity and compassion to flourish" (p. 77).

As faculty, we can make love work by taking time to balance our inner and outer lives. Work is important, but so is taking time for reflection and introspection as well as for rest and replenishment. We cannot make love work when lack of rest suppresses the reality of our private lives, including our emotions, our spirituality, and our relationships with our significant others. Stress and burnout diminish our capacity to be fully present in class, our ability to relate positively to students and colleagues, and our capacity to be creative with our work. Focusing solely on outer work does not give us the time to be in touch with our own lives, to be still in the vast territory of silence, and to reflect on the larger questions of life and why we do what we do. Sometimes, it is only when we experience a serious, life-altering crisis such as cancer, HIV/AIDS, or the death of a loved one that we realize the error of our ways. In *Tuesdays With Morrie* (Albom, 1997), a student asks Morrie, the ailing, dying professor, to speak about the most important questions of life. Morrie replies: "As I see it, they have to do with love, responsibility, spirituality, awareness. And if I were healthy today, those would still be my issues. They should have been there all along" (p. 175). We need to put a stop to waiting until we have a life-or-death crisis in order for us to have a spiritual awakening that points us to where we should have been all along. It can be very lonely and impoverishing to only be doing and not being.

We need to change the agreement that focusing only on outer work and its corollaries of stress, disease, and lack of intimacy is the preferred way to approach our work in higher education.

Example of newly revised agreement: *the agreement to balance our personal and professional lives with work, rest, and replenishment.*

The Agreement to Avoid Self-Examination

Engaging in the work of institutional transformation, such as creating a new dream of teaching and learning, can be exciting and fulfilling, yet difficult, painful, and frustrating. The examination of our own positionality is an important aspect when considering how to change what we do in the classroom—the curriculum, the way we engage with students, how we choose to share power, and so forth. Taking time to slow down and reflect is as important as spending time and energy in action to transform the institution. The work of transformation is not only about changing what is "out there"; it is about transforming what is "in here," our own internal views and assumptions. To what extent do I carry the oppressor within me? When I opt to do/say nothing, to what extent do I bring or perpetuate suffering to those who suffer from unjust institutional norms and values? How am I being changed by the work I do to create conditions of social justice? Yet, staying constantly busy with multiple projects works against self-reflexivity, which allows for noting what is happening inside of us as we engage the work of transformation (Gorski, 2000; Osei-Kofi et al., 2004). Often, when I have presented my ideas about transformation, I am told that this is exciting, yet I am asked: "Isn't this too much work? Doesn't this take up too much time?" If we ask these kinds of questions, we must also ask why we ask such questions. Questions about how we interpret our workload are as much questions of self-avoidance, fear, and resistance as they are about real commitment to engage in standing up to support our ethical and moral principles, a process that often evokes tension. How is it that we can spend so much time exhausting ourselves with multiple projects yet not make time for self-reflexivity? What are the deeper reasons we avoid confronting ourselves?

We need to change the agreement that taking time for introspection and addressing our own issues about transforming teaching and learning is unnecessary or "too much work."

Example of newly revised agreement: *the agreement to take time for self-reflexivity.*

An analysis of the dominant agreements that govern pedagogical practice in higher education takes us to the realization that we need to create an educational Dreamfield that reflects a re-created vision of reality. It is time to assemble and validate a pedagogical Dreamfield based on newly constructed agreements that speak to who we are as whole human beings—intelligent, social, emotional, and spiritual. Consequently, we need a committed group of educators interested in transformational change to recast the agreements that govern teaching and learning. This is not an easy task. It will take a significant amount of courage to work against entrenched agreements, the valor to step into the pain of admitting that we have been trying to transform higher education by working around these agreements rather than trying to change and recast the agreements themselves, and the bravery to admit that we have honored these agreements even when we knew, intuitively or intellectually, that some of the beliefs were flawed.

What is the experience of creating a new teaching and learning Dreamfield? In the next chapter, I introduce the faculty I interviewed to learn more about how they worked with a pedagogy of wholeness and harmony in the classroom.

2
Learning From Another's Story

It seems the ancient Medicine Men understood that listening to another's story somehow gives us the strength of example to carry on, as well as showing the aspects of ourselves we can't easily see. For listening to the stories of others— not to their precautions or personal commandments—is a kind of water that breaks the fever of our isolation. If we listen closely enough, we are soothed into remembering our common name.

—Nepo, 2000, p. 46

Invoking the question a Native American medicine man posed to the sick, "When was the last time you listened to the stories of others?" Nepo (2000) illuminates the power of presence and listening to truly learn from others. In listening we can experience a deep presence and recognize how at a very basic, even spiritual, level, sharing the stories of our humanity opens us to a deeper connection with others and ultimately with ourselves. As noted in the introduction, this book is based on a learning inquiry I undertook in which I interviewed 2- and 4-year college faculty to learn more about what they were doing to create a holistic teaching and learning context in their classrooms. In listening to the stories of my colleagues, I not only recognized our common purpose, but I was also inspired by their passion and courage. I remind readers that the core question guiding my inquiry was: What is the experience of creating a teaching and learning dream (pedagogic vision) based on wholeness and consonance, respecting the harmonious rhythm between the outer experience of intellectualism and rational analysis and the inner dimension of insight, emotion, and awareness?

The faculty I interviewed for this inquiry shared their stories, journeys, fears, and joy, and for that I am most grateful. Several were unaware that other faculty were engaging teaching and learning in similar ways. "Where are they?" one faculty member asked, perhaps reflecting on the notion that doing things differently is often risky and not shared with others, and that their kind of work was not openly discussed on campus. Nonetheless, I found them to be eager to speak about their work, and they felt energized with what they did with students. I gathered the strength to share my truth from listening and learning from their example. Their story is my story; this book is *our* book.

Faculty Interviews

In the appendix I provide a detailed account of the method I employed to conduct my study, and I briefly summarize my approach here. My learning inquiry used a purposeful sample (Denzin & Lincoln, 2000) of 15 faculty in higher education. A list of the participants is provided in Table 1. The faculty included 10 professors in 4-year and 5 in 2-year institutions. Of the 15 faculty, 7 were males, 10 were White, 3 were Latino/Latina, 1 was Asian, and 1 was African American. The key criterion I used to select faculty was that they had to have experience employing holistic teaching and learning practices that included some form of contemplative practice in their courses (e.g., reflection periods, journaling, artistic expression, etc.). I also sought diversity in terms of gender, race/ethnicity, discipline, and institutional type (e.g., 2- and 4-year college faculty). I conducted one-on-one, semistructured interviews with faculty, which lasted between one and two hours. When possible I interviewed some of their students in a focus-group setting.

Following heuristic (Moustakas, 1990) and transpersonal (Braud & Anderson, 1998) research methods, I positioned myself as a *coresearcher* with my interviewees, and I received my informants as partners and coresearchers who turned to one another in truth, while we attempted to open the interhuman

Table 1 Faculty Interview Participants

Name	Discipline	Institutional Type	Gender/Race/Ethnicity
Sam Tinsley	Mathematics	2-year	M/White
Rebecca Williams	Chemistry	2-year	F/White
Norma E. Cantú	English	4-year	F/Latina
Kristin B. Valentine	Communications	4-year	F/White
Mary F. Gibbons	English	2-year	F/White
Bill Neal	Physical Education	2-year	M/White
Alberto L. Pulido	Sociology	4-year	M/Latino
J. Herman Blake	African American Studies	4-year	M/African American
Susan Nummedal	Psychology	4-year	F/White
Xin Li	Education	4-year	F/Asian
Candace Kaye	Education	4-year	F/White
Barbara Jaffe	English	2-year	F/White
Robert London	Math Education	4-year	M/White
Sam Crowell	Education	4-year	M/White
Carlos Silveira	Art	4-year	M/Latino

Note: N = 15

nature of the experience. Heuristic inquiry is similar to the phenomenological approach that examines lived experiences and seeks to give them meaning. However, heuristics puts equal emphasis on the researcher and the people experiencing the phenomenon being studied. The researcher must have had the experience being explored. Transpersonal research methods seek to extend conventional views of the qualities and role of the researcher. Braud and Anderson indicate that the researcher's qualities, sensitivities, and being are important "in all phases of the research project" (p. 20), because ultimately it is through the researcher's filters that all study materials are "collected, processed, interpreted, and expressed" (p. 21). This methodological perspective was important, as it allowed me to engage my own experiences and those of my coresearchers.

Each faculty member received a formal invitation to be interviewed, including a copy of the interview protocol. Questions in the protocol related to the following: what brought them to the teaching profession, their philosophy of teaching and learning, the most important things they wanted students to learn, assessment practices, the nature of their relationships with students, incorporation of diversity in their courses, attending to individual and collective needs, powerful learning activities, use of contemplative practice activities, and obstacles to doing this kind of work. All except one coresearcher agreed to be videotaped, and all gave me permission to reveal their name and institutional affiliation.

The Faculty Members

The first four faculty I interviewed were teaching at Richland College, a 2-year institution in Dallas, Texas. Richland was unique because its principles related to establishing a community of learners with an emphasis on 10 values that are not usually overtly expressed in higher education's value system. Three of these values are as follows:

> WHOLENESS: We believe authentic people best *learn,* teach, serve, lead, and build community. Thus, our programs, services, and facilities nurture our unified mind-spirit-body and the emotional and intellectual intelligence requisite for meaningful lives.
>
> MINDFULNESS: We respect silence, using it for reflection and deeper understanding—not immediately filling silence with words after someone has spoken. We rush not to judgment but turn to wonder what was intended or being felt. Next, for clarity, we ask honest, open questions of others and ourselves.
>
> JOY: We value laughter, play, love, kindness, celebration, and joy in our learning and work—taking our learning and work seriously and ourselves lightly. (Richland College, 2007)

Richland College faculty were among the first to participate in the Fetzer Institute's Courage to Teach Program, which was built on the principles of teacher formation designed by Parker Palmer. These faculty members worked individually and collectively to explore the inner landscape of a teacher's life, and produced a series of essays captured in the monograph *To Teach With Soft Eyes: Reflections on the Teacher/Leaders Formation Experience* (García, 2000). The key principle of teacher formation is that all good teaching flows from the identity and integrity of the teacher, and that teachers teach who they are. Mary

Frances Gibbons, professor of English at Richland, expressed how the program changed her life:

> It gave us more of a look inward, and at who we are, and . . . [the experience] reaffirmed my knowledge that I really should be looking inward for what's important to me instead of externally. . . . Getting to Fetzer, seeing the beautiful natural setting, sitting there with my friends and colleagues in a quiet setting where there were no meetings to rush off to, no car pools to drive, no place to go, no traffic . . . just to sit and be with each other and learn about each other was a really very powerful and empowering experience for all of us.

I interviewed four faculty members at Richland College:

Mary Frances Gibbons expressed her teaching philosophy in the following manner:

> The whole purpose is for us to empower students, to look to who they really are, to look inward to find out who they really are, for them to remain true to what is important for them, for them to decipher through all this information they receive and pick and choose what really works for them.

When asked about her definition of spirituality, she said:

> Spirit to me is the essence of who I am. It's what works for me; it's being honest with myself, with others, and just following what seems right in my heart.

Sam Tinsley teaches mathematics at Richland, and had been a teacher for nearly 30 years at the time of our interview. He spoke of what spirituality meant for him:

> Spirituality . . . is defining my relationship with a higher being, with God if you would, and that spirituality takes on lots of dimensions. . . . trying

to understand who I am and how I relate to God and how I relate to other people . . . I think those are pretty inseparable.

Tinsley said it was difficult to incorporate the spiritual in mathematics, yet the teacher formation experience had made him more aware of "teaching who I am," no matter what material was being taught. He elaborated:

I am not afraid to say who my family is and talk about things that I experience and that are frustrating to me. . . . And in so doing I think students begin to see . . . this is a real person up there that's talking to me and not just a robot.

Rebecca Williams, who teaches chemistry at Richland, had been a teacher for 25 years when I interviewed her. She spoke of her spirituality as

connecting yourself to the whole and understanding . . . you've been in a grand scheme, a universe, and that it's how well those things fit together, and for me as a Christian . . . there's a relationship with God.

She also talked about her philosophy of teaching and learning, saying that teaching chemistry was a little more narrow than just teaching:

Teaching chemistry and learning chemistry [is] like taking a drink out of a fire hose, and that if I'm the teacher and I'm holding the hose and that the students somehow have to manage that hose system . . . I want to make sure that the students viewed . . . that there was more than one way to drink the water.

Bill Neal teaches physical education to seniors over the age of 50 at Richland, and at the time of our interview had been teaching for 38 years. He described his sense of spirituality as

an awareness of my belief system, the things that are important to me, the belief that there is something bigger, stronger, and mightier than myself that guides my life to a certain extent and also gives me strength to endure whatever activities or situations that come about within the course of my lifetime.

Philosophically, he said:

> Simply teaching the subject matter has never been satisfying enough for me. I think giving my students an opportunity to learn more about themselves to develop some lifetime skills to tie in many facets and factors of our lives within the framework of physical education and fitness all have become extremely important.

Neal's students nominated him for an outstanding teacher award, which he received.

Next I interviewed the following faculty:

Alberto López Pulido was teaching Latino and ethnic studies at Arizona State University, West Campus, at the time of our interview. After teaching at Brown University, Pulido was named director of ethnic studies at the University of San Diego in 2003. He is known for his research on the role of religion and the sacred in the Latino community. He is the author of *The Sacred World of the Penitentes* (2000), based on Los Hermanos Penitentes of New Mexico, a religious brotherhood in the Hispanic community. Pulido told me his life was a spiritual journey:

> I think it is a spiritual journey for me at a very, very deep, personal level. Because in terms of my own work and in terms of my own connections with people, I think that you are doing what you are doing for a reason and that to talk about my community, my culture and experiences—those are things that are deep inside of who I am, and so that in itself is a deeper form of spirituality because I am trying to embrace a deeper part of myself.

Responding to what he wanted students to take away from his class, he said:

> In a very kind of spiritual way, I am wanting them to remember the importance and the value of what was covered in the class in terms of decisions that they will be making as individuals and as professional people. . . . In

the end I would like to see some kind of change happening in our society from a larger perspective.

Norma Elia Cantú teaches English at the University of Texas, San Antonio, has also taught at Texas A&M University International, and has over 25 years of teaching experience. A distinguished feminist scholar and Latina folklorist, Cantú has an extensive list of publications, including *Canícula: Snapshots of a Girlhood en la Frontera* (1997), *Chicana Traditions: Continuity of Change* (2002), and *Telling to Live: Latina Feminist Testimonios,* edited by the Latina Feminist Group (2001). Cantú said that to serve and to teach were her life's tasks.

That's why I'm here; I feel very grounded in that belief that I am serving a higher purpose, a higher being.

When asked what she wanted her students to learn, she said:

I expect them to know the course content . . . and to know themselves, to have a sense of how they fit in the world.

Kristin B. Valentine, when I interviewed her, was teaching communications at Arizona State University, where she had been honored as a teacher-scholar no fewer than 12 times. She taught for 40 years before retiring. In 2002 Valentine received the Wallace A. Bacon Lifetime Teaching Excellence Award from the National Communication Association. Speaking about the spiritual nature of life, she said:

I find it comforting to know that I'm a very, very small little wet spot in the world. I don't need to see myself as the center of the universe. In fact I find that a bit scary.

On her philosophy of teaching and learning, she said:

I guess I teach the way I wish I had been taught and the way I know I learn, and I know there are lots of learning styles. So [in] my teaching, I try to hit as many as I can of these avenues of learning, figuring one or two of them are going to put the student in the center here, first.

J. Herman Blake is an emeritus professor with a distinguished career as a university administrator, in the positions of president, provost, and vice chancellor, and was a faculty member at the University of California, Santa Cruz; Tougaloo College; Vanderbilt University; Indiana University/Purdue University; and Iowa State University. The Carnegie Foundation named Blake the 2002 Iowa Professor of the Year. A fervent advocate for civil rights and high standards of excellence, Blake expressed his philosophy of teaching and learning in a simple, yet powerful statement:

> There is no known limit to the capacity of the human mind to learn, grow, develop, and change.

Susan Nummedal was teaching psychology at California State University, Long Beach, at the time of our interview, and is now retired. In 1999 she was selected to participate in the Carnegie Academy for the Scholarship of Teaching and Learning (CASTL) program. As a CASTL Scholar, she worked on a project to help students in a child development course think critically about diversity. Nummedal saw herself as a facilitator in the classroom. She said:

> While I'm aware that there are certain things that should be accomplished in a given course, I'm much more focused on what students bring to the setting. . . . the kinds of understanding, the kinds of experiences, the expectations that they have, and how we're going to work with those as we move towards some other stated goals. . . . These are the lenses through which they will be experiencing the class, and it is important for them—and for me—to be aware of them and how they affect learning as we move through the course. My favorite thing in the classroom is when I can really move out of the way of my students and let them be engaged collectively in some kind of discussion or an assignment or activity that they find meaningful.

She also told me that her Buddhist practice was deeply embedded in who she was and what she did.

Xin Li teaches intercultural education at California State University, Long Beach, and at the time of my interview had been teaching for 25 years. She is the author of *The Tao of Life Stories: Chinese Language, Poetry, and Culture in Education* (2002), focusing on her journey and the cross-cultural experiences of four other Chinese women. Li had started teaching in China during the Cultural Revolution, but she was exiled and told to work in the fields with local peasants in the mountains. This experience led to her passion for teaching and her understanding of privilege and lack of privilege in societal structures. When asked what she wanted her students to learn, she said, "to learn how to learn." She was engaged very deeply in the philosophy of Taoism.

Candace Kaye was teaching at California State University, Long Beach, when I interviewed her, and was responsible for the graduate program in early childhood education. Subsequently, she became a member of the graduate faculty in early childhood education at New Mexico State University. She was the recipient of a Contemplative Practice Fellowship cosponsored by the Center for Contemplative Mind in Society and the American Council on Learned Societies, with support from the Fetzer Institute and the Nathan Cummings Foundation. With the belief that greater insights into pedagogical practice and intellectual development can be stimulated through inwardness and silence, the fellowships allow individuals to develop courses and teaching materials that integrate contemplative practice. Speaking passionately about her philosophy of teaching, Kaye said:

> The core of my belief is the affect, the caring and the nurturing of the other. I am influenced primarily by Martin Buber and his philosophy of I and thou rather than I and it. . . . The thouness of the other human being that you are working with and the respect and the reciprocity of being in the same room with them. I also enjoy the dance, and I can't lead all the time, and I know, the classes when I lead and everyone else is following the energy, I am zapped at the end. But if I go in and I believe in sharing the energy so sometimes the students can lead . . . I have taught two-year-olds

through graduate students. I believe in the Dao of teaching. . . . when you enter the door of the classroom it is actually a Dao gate and you have to empty yourself of you in order to receive the students.

Barbara Jaffe was teaching English at El Camino Community College in Torrance, California, at the time of our interview. She was affiliated with the award-winning Puente Project that prepared low-income, first-generation college students to transfer to 4-year institutions and earn bachelor's degrees. Jaffe was passionate about teaching and her commitment to the betterment of society. She said:

I feel that on a daily basis I make a difference in a person's life. I think that every night I can go to sleep knowing I have tried to make this world a better place. I know that sounds trite, but that is what my father-in-law termed as psycho bucks. It may not be a monetary value, but psychologically, it makes me feel whole.

Robert London had been teaching mathematics education for 11 years at California State University, San Bernardino, when I interviewed him. His teaching load had been primarily in the master of arts program in holistic and integrative education, working with cohorts of master's students and focusing on clarifying the students' vision of education using a transformative model. He was also teaching elementary mathematics methods and research in education courses. In addition, he had over 20 years of teaching experience with grades 4 through high school, including 14 years as a high school mathematics teacher. He also served as an adjunct faculty member engaged in community work in low-income, urban areas. He expressed his teaching philosophy as follows:

I wouldn't label it as holistic or constructivist. I would say . . . particularly now in my life, I look at it from a spiritual perspective. . . . A guiding principle is to try to be sensitive to what is actually needed in a situation. . . . Another way of saying it is to try to be open to connecting with something larger, which I might label as spiritual. . . . To be able to see where there are times that something is driving your intent other than just your personality, or people telling you what you should be, or what you tell yourself you should be. Something I call source point, where we make a connection with something larger that I might label as spiritual, and we feel attracted to go into a particular direction.

London emphasized that while what he did on his own was important, the most valuable experiences were in his collaborations with other people. He was most satisfied, for example, with his collaborative efforts to develop a master's program in interdisciplinary studies that included an integrative education option, and his work with others to develop the Education and Spirituality Network, a directory of educators involved in exploring the role of religious diversity and spirituality in education. London had also been facilitating spirituality and education retreats for educators in higher education, two of which I attended at the James Reserve in California.

Sam Crowell is founder and co-coordinator of the master's program in integrative studies at California State University, San Bernardino. He has taught a wide range of courses, including Culture and Schooling, Social Foundations in Education, Expository Writing, Culture for Diverse Society, and Social Studies Methods. Crowell said that for a long time he viewed himself as being of service to the world. In terms of his teaching philosophy, he stated:

I see teaching as an applied philosophy . . . probably because I came out of philosophy. It is a way to investigate my world, my thoughts, and my ideas and reflect on those deeply, and reflect on those in terms of my practice and teaching and to reconsider my ideas philosophically as well. . . . If I were to characterize my philosophy, I guess I would be a constructive postmodernist. . . . I've been trying to understand the implications of the new sciences my whole higher education career and trying to apply those in some ways to the applied field of teaching. Within that there is a sense of recognizing and honoring the sense of wholeness in our world, the sense of interconnection and relationship. There is that sense of honoring and trying to trust the process, seeing things as not static, but always moving and always changing and transforming and having a sense that if we could somehow move beyond these ideas as just things to think about, and begin to live this particular vision that it might well make huge differences in our society and in our world and also as a person.

Carlos Silveira teaches art at California State University, Long Beach. Employing the philosophical framework of Paulo Friere, Silveira employed community service learning as a pedagogical tool to teach art. Modeling the import of community service learning, he traveled to Brazil to help poor children in *favelas* (shantytowns) learn art through an antiracist curriculum. California State University, Long Beach, honored Silveira with the 2003–04 Community Service Learning Faculty Fellow Award. In 2001 he received the J. Paul Getty Service Learning Scholar Award. Silveira understands that teaching and learning transcend a focus on content. He said:

> I think [students] have to be, first of all, humanitarians as teachers. They have to develop this sense of compassion nowadays that is extremely important in teaching. Of course the theory is [also] extremely important in the classroom.

Now that I have introduced the reader to the faculty whose collective experiences serve as the foundation for creating a new pedagogical Dreamfield, in the next chapter I describe the creation of an integrative, consonant pedagogy.

3

Refashioning the Dream

THE EXPERIENCE OF CREATING AN INTEGRATIVE, CONSONANT PEDAGOGY

Education, to me, is not theory. It is not requirements. It is not lesson plans. Education is felt. It is shared. It is a commitment to all the children of the earth and to all the flora and fauna of the planet. It is the realization that holistic learning, spiritual practices, and sacred space are not elements to shy away from or fear, but instead are the bonds that hold all of us together.
—Donnelly, 2002, p. 311

"Teach for life, not for death," the Aztec elder told me. "Maintain life; obey the natural laws of life." As in the opening quote from John Donnelly, the Aztec elder was expressing the importance of maintaining a commitment to do only those things that keep us present and alive, and to do everything to reconstruct what is not in harmony. In this chapter I illuminate what faculty did to create a new pedagogical vision based on two themes: (a) integration, the unitive elements of what appear to be solely oppositional concepts, and (b) consonance, the harmony that exists between two complementary concepts. As noted on pp. 26–33 in chapter 1, one of the agreements held in mass consciousness is that intellectual reasoning and emotion are polar opposites—that is, the mind is usually understood to be totally and always separate from the internal experience.

However, an integrative, consonant approach would attempt to see how the mind and feelings are connected and how they work together in a natural rhythm that respects their distinctiveness, yet appreciates their complementarity. An education that keeps us present and alive is one that seeks to challenge our dualistic belief systems based on either/or frameworks and to work with the whole person with balanced attention to intellectual, social, and spiritual development. Educators who work with a nondualistic framework can fashion a new reality about teaching and learning in their classrooms.

In the next sections I focus on (a) a depiction of non-Western, anticolonial epistemological and ontological perspectives that serve as a foundation for the integrative, consonant pedagogy that emerged from this study; (b) the use of the Aztec literary device called *difrasismo;* and (c) the first pedagogical position that evolved from the study.

Non-Western Epistemological and Ontological Perspectives

When we separate ourselves from our internal experience by objectifying things in order to categorize and intellectualize them, we override the informative signals of body, heart, and mental imagery, all of which creates doubt regarding our own internal experience. Clearly, we need different kinds of information, but our cultural way of placing attention is too heavily stacked in favor of the outer senses of seeing and hearing and the tendency toward rational analysis.
—Charles H. Simpkinson, *publisher,* Common Boundary *magazine*

What is the epistemological and ontological framework that becomes a substructure for a pedagogy based on consonance and connectedness? My learning inquiry was concerned with employing a non-Western, anticolonial epistemological foundation (Dei & Kemph, 2006; Tuhiwai Smith, 1999) based on indigenous knowledge.

Epistemology and Ontology

In the world of philosophy, epistemology refers to a theory of knowledge. Epistemological questions might include, What is knowledge? How is knowledge assessed? What constitutes valid knowledge? How do we know what we know? Is knowledge acquired through the senses or through reason? Epistemology is often contrasted with ontology, which refers to the nature of being. The separateness logic of Western epistemology privileges rationalism as a way of knowing and separates it from intuition. Dominant Western ways of knowing divorce epistemology from ontology and separate the subject from the object that is being studied (Moodie, 2004; Tarnas, 1998). Yet, ancient wisdom and many spiritual traditions articulate a different truth, an epistemology based not on separation but on wholeness, not on the disconnection but the union of the knower and what is to be known, not on the polarization of faith and reason but on the unitive nature of science and the divine. The ontology of many indigenous cultures, such as the Mayas and Aztecs, as well as Aboriginal, American Indian/Alaska Native, Asian, and African worldviews, expresses the nature of humanity as seeking belonging, as being in community with others and with the world. Descartes' philosophical stance of "I think, therefore I am," is contrasted with "I belong, therefore I am" (Moodie).

The ontological stance of belonging and being connected to others and to the world is a thread of thought found in expressions such as the American Indian articulation "to all my relations" and "uMuntu ngumuntu ngabantu," the isiZulu version meaning "a person is a person because of the people" (Moodie, 2004, p. 4). In the Aztec worldview Ometeotl represented the supreme God of duality who joined male and female principles. This is similar to the Chinese construction of yin and yang as complementary opposites that cannot exist without each other. For Mesoamerican cultures such as the Maya and the Aztecs, the principle of duality was not an absolute either/or concept. The principle involved the use of paired oppositions, while recognizing that two opposites are interdependent and supportive of each other, that is, male-female, day-night, earth-sky (Miller & Taube, 1993; Tedlock, 1996).

Difrasismo *as a Literary Device*

León-Portilla (1963) noted that Ángel María Garibay K. identified one of the most fascinating stylistic traits found in Aztec ritual speech, which he called *difrasismo,* a literary device in which a pair of seemingly opposite terms was used to refer to a third concept or phrase. To give an idea maximum clarity and precision, two of its qualities were isolated and then paired to form a single metaphoric unit. For example, fire and water could be employed to allude to war, red and black ink to writing, or night and wind for the transcendency of the divine. The third term in the difrasismo revealed the hidden gift of the wisdom in the paired dualities, for example, I.you.belong and sky.earth.world. Only when one critically analyzed the double term could its complete meaning be established. The difrasismo *in xochitl in cuicatl* (flowers and song) was employed to refer to poetry and all artistic endeavors imbued with beauty. For the Aztecs, the only truth on earth was poetic and beautiful, like flowers and song (Miller & Taube, 1993; León-Portilla, 1963). The Nahuatl people employed these expressions in a metaphorical fashion; if taken literally, their meaning was distorted or lost (León-Portilla, 1963).

A difrasismo may be considered a dialectical space where new understandings might emerge through the integration of polarities. Hidden within dualities is a dynamic, integrative center, which, once unlocked, unveils a larger reality. Unlocking the polarities requires surrendering old belief systems and working with our growth edges as we begin to uncover a larger truth that joins two realms of reality. I employ the Aztec stylistic concept of difrasismo to elucidate two pedagogical positions that emerged from faculty interviews:

- Position I: Employing an Integrative, Consonant Pedagogy
- Position II: Employing an Integrative, Consonant Pedagogy Rooted in Social Justice

I present these two positions not to create a hierarchy of preference or pedagogical sophistication, as both positions are quite meaningful and appropriate depending on the readiness of the professor and students to engage in specific teaching and learning processes. Rather, the intent is to provide examples of different beginning points for faculty who are interested in engaging an integrative, consonant pedagogy.

It is also not my intention to put faculty in a particular "box" with the positions. While it is possible that some faculty operated in one single position, it is also quite likely that faculty were able to move back and forth between positions depending on what was being taught and what the aim of the course was. It is also possible that faculty understood, at least intuitively, that not every pedagogical approach can be appropriate all the time and in every classroom situation. Pedagogical choice relies on context, preparedness, purpose, and receptivity. Accordingly, faculty teach "for the moment," not for a universal norm (Barndt, 1989; Matthews, 2005). For each pedagogical position I provide examples of teaching and learning approaches and describe the difrasismos that serve as the foundation of each position. In this chapter I discuss the first position that evolved from this study. Chapter 4 focuses on Position II.

Position I:
Employing an Integrative, Consonant Pedagogy

In Position I, faculty appeared to operate with two assumptions: (a) that inner and outer learning are connected and (b) that contemplative practice is important to engage the learner deeply in the learning material. Faculty recognized that inner learning (i.e., working with emotion, reflective processes, subjective views, etc.) and outer learning (i.e., working with intellectual activities such as reasoning, problem solving, learning, academic concepts, etc.) should be integrated, as opposed to being separate and apart. Faculty appeared to appreciate the complementarity and rhythm between inner and outer learning and found ways and means to combine both processes to ensure that the material was being covered, that students were employing high-level mental processes, and that students were reflecting on the larger meaning of what was being studied.

Faculty also operated with the principle of connectedness where the learner was viewed as being able to engage with the course material in a deeper fashion through the use of contemplative practices. Faculty understood that diverse forms of contemplative practice could be effectively employed as tools to allow students to engage more deeply with what was being learned, to complement and embellish intellectual learning, and to foster the acquisition of knowledge from the course material, as well as to connect with inner wisdom.

Definition of Contemplative Practice

Before elaborating further on the first position that emerged, it is appropriate to provide a definition of contemplative practice. The Center for Contemplative Mind in Society (2007) offers a working definition of contemplative practice:

Contemplative practices quiet the mind in order to cultivate a personal capacity for deep concentration and insight. Examples of contemplative practice include not only sitting in silence but also many forms of single-minded concentration, including meditation, contemplative prayer, mindful walking, focused experiences in nature, yoga, and other contemporary physical or artistic practices. We also consider various kinds of ritual and ceremony designed to create sacred space and increase insight and awareness to be forms of contemplative practice.

Further, the Center notes:

Contemplative practice has the potential to bring different aspects of one's self into focus, to help develop personal goodness and compassion, and to awaken an awareness of the interconnectedness of all life. They [these practices] have helped people develop greater empathy and communication skills, improve focus and concentration, reduce stress, and enhance creativity. Over time, these practices cultivate insight, inspiration, and a loving and compassionate approach to life. They are practical, radical, and transformative.

Similarly, Naropa University (2008), whose mission is contemplative education, presents the following definition on its Web site:

Contemplative education is learning infused with the experience of awareness, insight and compassion for oneself and others, honed through the practice of sitting meditation and other contemplative disciplines. The rigor of these disciplined practices prepares the mind to process information in new and perhaps unexpected ways. Contemplative practice unlocks the power of deep inward observation, enabling the learner to tap into a wellspring of knowledge about the nature of mind, self and other that has been largely overlooked by traditional, Western-oriented liberal education.

The Center for Contemplative Mind in Society (2007) created a Tree of Contemplative Practices, with seven categories of practices to cultivate awareness and to develop a stronger connection to inner wisdom. Employing the categories of this tree, some of these practices that were used by faculty I interviewed included (a) *stillness practices,* such as moments of silence and meditation; (b) *movement practices,* such as walking, hiking, and communing with nature; (c) *creation process practices,* such as contemplative art, photographs, music, and poetry; (d) *activist practices,* such as community work where social justice themes are highlighted; (e) *generative practices,* such as love, kindness, and compassion; (f) *ritual/cyclical practices,* such as creating a sacred space and rituals based on cultural and religious traditions; and (g) *relational practices,* such as storytelling, autobiography, free writing, journaling, dialogue, and deep listening. In the next section I offer specific examples of how faculty employed an integrative, consonant pedagogy.

Examples From Faculty of an Integrative, Consonant Pedagogy

In the classrooms of the faculty I interviewed, contemplative practice could be as simple as having students walk around a lake before writing, journaling about their fears of mathematics, going on a hike, writing poetry, playing music as a backdrop for class, or sitting in silence for a few minutes. However, some faculty clearly had developed more in-depth approaches that allowed for greater focusing and attention to generate greater insight and awareness of the subject matter and to guide the student's relationship with what was being learned.

Employing Storytelling, Photographs, and Music to Explore African American History

J. Herman Blake was passionately interested in setting high standards of academic excellence in his African American studies courses. Moreover, Blake infused a contemplative dimension into course assignments through the use of what the Center for Contemplative Mind in Society (2007) calls creation process practices, such as contemplative art, photos, and music. Blake pushed his students to excel beyond their perceived limits. He spoke eloquently about setting high standards for learning:

> So it's a 15-week course, 16 weeks with finals and all that. You've got to read 16 books. . . . they're all biographies and autobiographies, but you've got to read them all. All 16 in their entirety, there's no reader, and you've got to write 13 papers, and from the second week on when you come into the classroom you're going to get an assignment. You've got to write an essay on it, and the assignment is always harder, larger than the amount of time.

You can't complete it in 30 minutes, but you've got to write it. Two things happen: One, you learn how to organize your ideas and deliver them more effectively in that 30 minutes, and two, you walk out of there thinking about all the things you could have said. When you walk out of here thinking about all the things you could have said, it keeps you thinking, it keeps you learning.

Blake continued:

There are two or three, sometimes as many as four times a semester you have to lead the discussion, but you've got to bring a paper. You can't come and say I thought of this; you've got to focus on the classroom material; you've got to lead the discussion. . . . And I evaluate the paper; I evaluate everything. . . . So you've got these 13 essays you've got to write on assigned topics; you've got these three or four papers you've got to write to lead the discussion; you've got these 16 books you've got to read. Right? Then you come to the end of the semester, you get this comprehensive examination, which is a take home, which could take a week, and you've got a weekend. There are students who come back 2 or 3 years later and tell me they're still working with the material!

Over time, Blake developed a reputation for having rigorous, demanding, academic classes. However, Blake engaged his students in more than academic work. He spoke about how he employed contemplative tools such as storytelling, photographs, and music to connect students with the material at deeper levels:

I use in the class some of my own material, my own research, I have them listen to, for example, when I talk about slavery, I have them listen to an interview done in 1968 with a woman whose mother was a breeder, and it was her mother's job to have babies. And this woman talks. She was the 15th child of this woman, born just after peace [was] declared, as she put it. She was, I think 94, 98, something like this, and I have a picture of her, which I share along with the transcript. I want to tell you, you can't hear that and walk away without thinking. When I get to talking about terrorism and violence I use about six or seven slides from that book *Without Sanctuary* (Allen, 2000), then I raise two questions: Why do they lynch people? And then I show the pictures of the crowds who came to enjoy the spectacle, including young children, and one student wrote an essay saying, "This course is not only about learning, this course is about thinking and you think all the time." I use music, because the music was used by the people, to illustrate these points. So when they hear this woman whose mother was a breeder, I play for them the spiritual "Lord How Come Me Here, I Wish I Never Was Born." When they see those slides about how people have been misused and mistreated, I have them listen to Nina Simone singing "Strange Fruit."

In Blake's class, students not only completed an assignment but also returned to it to reflect, rewrite, and resubmit. The process fostered constant student engagement. Blake elaborates:

So out of one side you're doing this intellectual academic thing and the other side you're doing this personal thing. And you're going to hook it up. I am not going to hook it up for you! You're going to hook it up. And I don't know when it's going to happen, but as long as you're working with me you are going to be continuing to do this reflection. That introspection or reflection, I mean that's [a] constant process of learning because you don't do it and then stop. You do it and when you least think about it something comes to you, and students aren't used to just constantly being in a learning mode.

Blake's students spoke highly of him as a professor and mentor. Some talked about having acquired a sense of purpose in their lives. One woman related a story that another student had told her about the transformation taking place in Blake's students. The student told her, "I can't believe at 38 years old I'm finding out so many things that took place in my own country. . . . I'm hearing from how [Blake's] class has really transformed [students'] lives, made them reflect more about their family or their philosophy of their community or where they came from."

A male student came upon the following revelation after watching the slides of people being lynched and hearing the song "Strange Fruit": "I consider myself a humanitarian, so I want to change the world. I want to better the world, and it [the class] motivated me. . . . since I'm African American . . . I feel like . . . I've got to do something, I have to." Another student was dealing with issues related to difference and racism for the first time in her life.

Using Journaling to Engage More Deeply in Curriculum Development

Candace Kaye spoke about a particularly powerful assignment when she asked students to keep a "moon journal." As a contemplative relational practice tool (Center for Contemplative Mind in Society, 2007), the moon journal was employed to foster student reflection and to complete an academic assignment that required students to generate a curriculum based on children's stories. The pairing of a curriculum development assignment with a contemplative dimension resulted not just in understanding and completing the assignment, but also in fostering a reflective process that embellished and deeply illuminated the nature of the assignment. Kaye said:

> This summer I had [students] keep a moon journal based on the work of Penny Oldfather. I taught a beginning course for the cohort out of the professional development school. It was a constructivist process, and to get them in touch with understanding constructivist pedagogy, I had them keep a moon journal, and they were to go out and look at the moon every night. And I timed it, and it was lucky, the first night there was no moon. And so they went through this process of being really annoyed with me. And I said I want you to write whatever you want to, and they were looking for the moon and they kept a journal, and then the moon started appearing, and they had to do this for the whole time of the summer session.

Kaye continued:

> And then out of this they created curriculum. And what I wanted them to learn . . . was a metaphor for the idea that you start with this nothing sky that you don't know anything, and you've got to know something because it is an assignment. And then you get to the point that you are fully illuminated

with this full moon. And what they did with this learning, they then created a constructivist-based curriculum on the moon for their classroom. And out of that curriculum, they were divided into groups. There was one group who had their total curriculum based on folktales about the moon and the children's stories. . . . It was powerful because they were reflective just like the moon is from the very beginning. . . . it was an amazing experience!

Involving Students in a Retreat Setting
to Gain Awareness About Teaching Mathematics

Robert London involved his master's students in weekend retreats at the James Reserve in the San Jacinto Mountains in Idyllwild, California. In this secluded, mountainous setting filled with hundreds of plant and animal species, students could engage in contemplative movement practices such as walking, hiking, and communing with nature (Center for Contemplative Mind in Society, 2007). In addition, he taught a section of Elementary Mathematics Methods primarily at this setting—two weekends at the reserve and two classes on campus. In a research study comparing this section with a section of the same class taught entirely on campus, London found a significant difference in the students' perception of the effect of the learning environment on their learning. On a 7-point Likert scale, 75% of the students in the reserve setting identified the class setting in nature as the most positive postsecondary course learning environment. The remaining 25% ranked the course in the top 25% of postsecondary courses. Most of the control group, as expected, rated the on-campus classroom environment in the middle, with a few to the left and right of the middle.

Student comments suggested that the environment was very relaxing, as well as conducive to reflection. The outdoors became incorporated into the mathematics curriculum and into students' reflective processes. London said that "it was easy to connect with spirit here" because the setting allowed students to look more deeply at what they were doing as teachers, as well as to discover the hidden teacher in themselves. Here, London guided students into diverse approaches to teaching mathematics and allowed them to take methods that appealed to them, experiment with them, reflect on what was learned, and come back to share reflections and methods with the group. A major emphasis of the course was teaching the students to plan and implement a cooperative group activity that employed manipulatives and focused on problem solving. London emphasized that a major component of becoming an effective educator was understanding what one already believed about effective teaching from one's own experiences, staying connected to those understandings, and deepening them through reflection and further experimentation. For example, students were shown a videotape of a fourth grade teacher who implemented a holistic approach to education over an entire school year. In this instance, the major theme of the school year was the pilgrims. At the beginning of the year, students came into an empty classroom and had to design and construct their desks using tools the pilgrims had access to at the time. Students raised funds through shareholders in the community to allow for the various projects and provided the shareholders with a weekly newsletter on their activities. They also hosted special events such as plays and performances. Throughout the year the students had meaningful input into the process of their education and were required to solve problems that naturally arose through their school projects. The videotape included interviews with students, parents, and community members 2 years later. London's college students who watched the video were assigned to pick one aspect of the teacher's teaching approach, to try an experiment involving teaching mathematics, and to reflect on the experiment. Each student picked a different aspect reflecting his or her present understanding of what was important in teaching. For example, some students focused on increasing student input in their classroom, while others focused on integrating problem solving, group work, or the arts in their classroom. The class discussion of the experimentation provided a rich context for exploring holistic approaches to teaching mathematics.

Employing *Cajitas* to Explore Culture and Identity

Alberto Pulido (2004) said that one of his most important teaching objectives

> is to recognize and account for the intersection of academic intellectual knowledge with that of everyday experience. . . . When this occurs, then I believe they will recognize the importance of how their work interacts with the real life issues and problems in their lives. (p. 73)

When I asked Pulido to talk about some of the most powerful moments in his ethnic studies classes, he was excited to speak about his *cajitas* (sacred boxes) project. In their sacred boxes, students pay tribute to their families, honor loved ones who have passed away, and make political statements. Students also compose a one-page essay to articulate the meaning of their artistic and highly personal creations. The cajitas project is an example of employing practices that involve creation of sacred space and the use of rituals associated with cultural and religious traditions (Center for Contemplative Mind in Society, 2007). Pulido showed me one of his student's cajitas called "My Life as a Meztiza," and said,

> The discussions that we had about [the cajita] are that [this student] considers herself to be part Chicana and part Apache. And when you look at the imagery . . . you see some of the traditional symbols of what it means to be Mejicana or Chicana. Then you see Christian symbols and Native American symbols. Up on top . . . there is an actual . . . agricultural field. There is an eagle that has been carved in. There's a horse, there's some Native American symbols as well. And I think it captures those dualities and living in multiple worlds.

For Pulido, life was like a never-ending journey of discovery. He said that he was particularly interested in breakthroughs:

> I am very interested in . . . people breaking through, people finding some answer, and some revelation at whatever level. And they can be really small or they can be life changing. And what I find really important is that I really think that is what I am also doing.

The cajitas project appeared to stimulate some of these breakthrough, insightful moments of learning. For one student, his breakthrough came as he was constructing a cajita based on his deceased father. In the process of constructing his cajita, the student said that he had gotten more in touch with his father's life, and now asked:

What would he want me to do? What could I do that would impress him or make him come back, so to speak? And when he, when he departed it's like, there's nothing that I could have done; no, nothing that I could have done at that time. And for me the project was powerful in that it made me examine him more closely, find out and question what he lived his life like.

Another student commented on how the cajitas project had elicited emotion and had fostered the development of his identity:

You have to express yourself emotionally. . . . No one else is helping you but yourself. . . . *La cajita* is yours and no one . . . They are not going to understand it the way that you are going to understand it because those are your feelings, those are your emotions, those are your thoughts. . . . in my cajita . . . I found myself. I found my identity.

He continued:

When I came and I presented [the cajita] . . . I left it open, and, and I left it to discussion, and I let people who wanted to hear the story behind it. I let them find me and then I shared the story. And then when, when you share the story you can't put every little detail, but I put enough detail where they found the substance of the story and they understood . . . [the cajita] and theory transformation, and finding your identity, and sharing it with people who, who want to know . . . That was probably the most . . . influential assignment that I have ever had.

Employing Cajitas to Connect
Academic Research to Student Identity

I borrowed the concept of cajitas to use in my advanced research methods course with doctoral students who were in the process of writing their dissertation proposal in an educational leadership program cosponsored by the University of California, Irvine, and California State University, Long Beach. In this course I taught research methods and assisted students in completing their dissertation proposals; the first three chapters of their dissertation, which included the statement of the problem; literature review; and method. It became apparent to me that the topics these students were choosing to investigate were very close to their lived experiences. For example, one student who was a school administrator was studying the concept of distributed leadership in schools. Another, who worked with student athletes, was studying the impact of new academic regulations on athletes. Yet another was exploring African American female spirituality. My goal was for students to see the connection between what they were learning and who they are, for it was apparent to me that what we choose to study is deeply rooted in our identity. To meet the academic requirements of the course, we covered several quantitative and qualitative research methods, and students were asked to submit their dissertation proposals. In addition I had them construct a research cajita, and I told them that I would create a cajita as well. Although I told my students that they could construct the cajita in any way they chose, I did ask them to include artifacts that represented

- their ontology, the way they viewed the nature of humanity,
- who or what influenced them to engage in their particular line of inquiry,
- what their research meant to them,
- their perceived strengths and limitations, and
- how they hoped their research would make a difference.

In one of the last sessions of the course, we each took turns in presenting our research cajitas and sharing our stories—the journey of coming to a place where we were now scholars, researchers engaged in illuminating truth. It is important to note here that the cajita presentations were made after the class had an opportunity to bond and when the class participants felt a sense of trust and support for one another. Spontaneously, students clapped after each cajita presentation. By the time we were through, there was not a dry eye in the class. Students spoke about joyful and traumatic events in their lives. One student wondered how she could fully do justice to the individuals she interviewed because her lived experience was so different. She spoke about how she was on a journey trying to figure out who she was. Another spoke about the dialectic of being part of a privileged ethnicity (White male), while being part of a stigmatized social group (gay). I spoke of my brutally murdered uncle, whose name I carry, my upbringing in poverty, and my having arrived in a privileged academic space where I wanted to make a difference for students who, like me, grow up with hopes and dreams but do not know how to realize them.

Although sharing our stories created tension at times (partly because we have been taught to suppress emotions in the classroom), we held each other in our collective vessel of caring and support. This turned out to be the most powerful moment of the course, and I was very pleased with my student evaluations. Students appreciated the opportunity both to learn more about research methods and to engage in reflection. For example, one student wrote: "The cajitas project was an opportunity to self reflect that allowed me to search inside myself for the reasons I am in the program. Also, the research/method review was absolutely relevant to my research process." Another said that "the cajitas had to be the most meaningful and powerful assignment I have ever done!"

Employing Photographs as a Meditative Tool
to Connect Content to Personal Experience

Norma Cantú incorporated creation process practices through the use of photographs and relational practices, such as storytelling and autobiography (Center for Contemplative Mind in Society, 2007), as meditative tools to connect content to personal experience. Cantú herself had employed photographs of her childhood to create a tender, yet powerful autobioethnographic novel called *Canícula: Snapshots of a Girlhood en la Frontera* (Cantú, 1997). She articulated how the photos and guided imagery exercises helped students enter a learning zone that was deeper than simply writing about their experiences.

Whenever we work with writing, we're really working with spiritual things, and even before I ever wrote *Canícula,* I used to have an exercise for my students to remember a photograph of themselves as children and write about it. And I'm teaching description and sentence combining and all that stuff, but I have them do these guided imagery exercises. . . . And one student was writing and it gets very emotional [because the writing is] about themselves and their families. . . . But I guide them; we start with things that are more innocuous until we get to something that is more personal. . . . They wrote [the paper] and went home. They take [the paper] home, they read it in their small group; they take it home, revise, edit, and then turn it in to get a grade. And this one student came back. . . . and she said, "I cried all night. . . . You have helped me to know my mother." I had asked them to write, and the picture she remembered was of her mom and her.

Cantú continued:

> She with her kids, her siblings, are all huddled around her mother. . . . So she wrote about that picture and then she started talking to the mother. So *no durmio* [she didn't sleep], and she was up working on that paper all night, and came back the next morning and told me this and was so grateful. . . . I can't take credit and say I did it. I allowed it to happen, and those are the kinds of moments, and this is just one example of how something works, even if I probably didn't have much to do with it except setting it up and then it happened.

Use of Meditative Ritual to Demystify Writing

Cantú understood that many of her students whose first language was not English had difficulties in writing, and she designed a ritual to help eliminate their fears. The ritual created a meditative space that allowed students to get in touch with their inner feelings about writing and to release their fears and move beyond them. By liberating students from these fears, she hoped that writing could be demystified and that students could begin to write, feeling more confident about themselves and their writing ability. Cantú spoke to me about this ritual:

> I was teaching linguistics and these students just absolutely hated it. They're insecure because it's about English. . . . It's like a brand new language, and it is. So I said, you're going to master it. But they are so scared, and they have all these horror stories. The first day everybody gives their name and why [they were enrolled] in the class—Well, because it's required. I hate language, I hate grammar. So . . . I had them think about this and write down three fears. Why are you afraid of it? What makes you afraid of grammar? Well, I'm afraid of making a mistake. You hate it? Yeah. What is it that you hate about it? So we wrote them down and then we twisted them up. It was anonymous, nobody knew. I put them in a stainless steel bowl.

Cantú continued her story:

> So we went into my backyard and I said: OK, we're going to build a fire and we are going to burn these hates and fears away and visualize them just going up into smoke. They are ashes and they are no longer yours, and you don't have that anymore. You should have seen them. They were crying. Some of them had tears in their eyes when they were writing. . . . I can't tell you that all of them got an A+, but it helped [them] go to the next [level].

Employing Meditation to Help Students Gain Greater Awareness of Identity

The Center for Contemplative Mind in Society (2007) identifies meditation as a stillness practice that can foster deep concentration and insight. In a Student Development Theory course I taught at California State University, Long Beach, for master's students preparing to be student affairs administrators I found myself with a unique challenge. How could I infuse contemplative elements into a course on theory? What I began to do was to meditate in the afternoons before class met. I began to realize that the course I was teaching, which involved covering many theories regarding how students develop their identity in college, was simply dealing with a time-honored question of the soul—Who am I? And so I informed my students that on one particular evening we would be doing something out of the ordinary; we would be spending one hour in silence reflecting on the question, Who am I? I told the students that there was no one way to reflect, that they could bring pillows, sit on the floor or on their desks, and that at the end of the hour I would ring a bell and we would spend 15 minutes doing free writing to articulate what we had learned from our reflection. I participated in the entire activity with my students. I was careful to tell them that this kind of activity might elicit emotions that could make some uncomfortable. Consequently, students who felt they could not participate in this exercise were excused from the class on this particular day. All but one student, who later came to my office to explain that she was dealing with some difficult personal issues, came to class.

To prepare these students for this reflective activity, I asked them to read Wayne Muller's (1997) book, *How, Then Shall We Live?*—an insightful work that deals with the spirituality of identity. Muller notes that four simple questions shape the spiritual journey of individuals: Who am I? What do I love? How shall I live, knowing I will die? What is my gift to the family of this earth? Muller explains that the search for our identity is fundamental, and that the truth about our essence is within us. We spent the hour in silence, followed by 15 minutes of free writing. We then took a break, and I brought pizza and soft drinks. We spent the next hour reflecting and sharing what we had learned. I was pleased and amazed at how students embraced this activity. Here are some examples of the comments students made:

- "I loved [the professor's] incorporation of spiritual themes. She challenged us to think beyond the curriculum, reflect, grow and develop personally."
- "This class has been a phenomenal experience for me. I have enjoyed all the spiritual and reflective aspects of the class that could have potentially been just intellectual and dry. [The professor] brought life into the theories and encouraged [students] to reflect."
- "I have learned more about myself and my personal development than in any other class."
- "This class was phenomenal with its reflective elements. I didn't know theory could be this lively and interesting."

Faculty Positionality

A teaching and learning approach that is integrative and harmonic requires attention to the positionality of the instructor. The faculty I interviewed positioned themselves not so much as experts but as facilitators of learning and as "real people." Gibbons explains:

I think I have a really good relationship with the students. I think one reason why my relationship is very good is that I try to be nonthreatening. . . . Also, being a guide at the site rather than a sage on the stage I think helps because I get out among the students. I relate to them on [a] one-on-one basis. [Also] the nature of their writing in this course, and the topics they select, often give me insight into who they are and what their lives are like, and so I can communicate with them on those terms too.

Further, most faculty spoke about the importance of bringing who they were to class. They appeared comfortable sharing stories about their families, cultural experiences, and ups and downs of life. In this fashion, the classroom served as a way to invite not only the expertise of the professor but also the voice of the students. Some faculty allowed students to call them by their first name. Others viewed students as colleagues and as fellow learners. Letting go of the position of being the sole expert, allowing students to shape their own learning, and inviting personal experience represented ways to decenter the power relationships in the classroom. The effect was that students and teachers met each other on a more equal plane, not so much as teacher to student but as human to human.

Difrasismos Inherent in Integrative, Consonant Pedagogy

What is the epistemological framework that serves as the foundation for Position I? Faculty operating in Position I broke the agreement of separation discussed on pp. 33–36 in chapter 1 to create a teaching and learning Dreamfield that embraced connectedness. Two frameworks emerged:

1. The first framework may be captured in the following difrasismo: Object.Subject.Participatory Epistemology, which reflects the connection between the object (material to be studied) and subject (student), as well as the fact that when the object and the subject come together, the result is a participatory epistemology (see Figure 1).
2. The second framework is reflected in the following difrasismo: Content.Contemplation.Knowledge/Wisdom, which illuminates the relationship between content (the material to be studied) and contemplation (the use of diverse forms of contemplative practice). This relationship facilitated the generation of knowledge and wisdom (see Figure 2). Next, I elaborate on each of these frameworks.

Figure 1 Stances Reflecting the Relationship Between Object and Subject

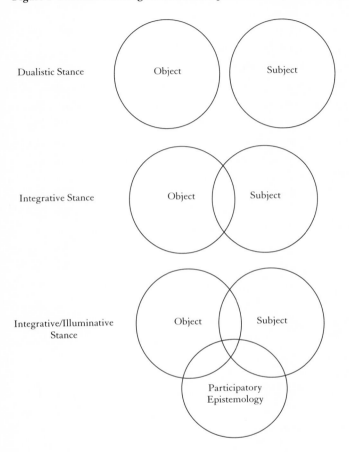

The Relationship Between the Content and Student

Figure 1 depicts three epistemological stances regarding the relationship between the student and the material to be learned.

DUALISTIC. This stance employs a separatist, dualistic framework where the human learner views the subject matter as an objective, emotionless spectator, not as a participant actively engaged in learning. Dualism is reflective of the agreement of separation discussed on pp. 33–36 in chapter 1. Faculty appeared to stay away from operating with a dualistic framework.

INTEGRATIVE. In the integrative stance the object and the subject come together. Students are fully connected to what they are learning, and an epistemological framework that is unitive in nature is employed. While faculty did employ an integrative framework to teaching and learning, it is also helpful to see beyond the connection of the student and the subject matter, as something more expansive appeared to be occurring within that union.

INTEGRATIVE/ILLUMINATIVE. I believe that what faculty were doing in the classroom can best be captured in the integrative/illuminative stance, reflected in the difrasismo Object.Subject.Participatory Epistemology. Here, the learner and subject matter are united, but the difrasismo also illuminates the hidden gift in the relationship. The union of the learner and the subject matter results in a participatory epistemology, "the knowing that occurs when the perceiver and the perceived are united as a single consciousness" (Lachman, 1998, p. 8). Drawing from his work on peak learning experiences, Maslow (1988) explains that in these moments, the learner "loses his past and his future for the time being and lives totally in the here-now experience. He is 'all there,' immersed, concentrated, fascinated" (p. 83). The difrasismo captures the integrative, harmonic dynamics that exist between the learner and what is being studied. In a participatory epistemology, the learner is deeply connected to what is being learned. The tools to generate this deep engagement are diverse forms of contemplative practice, such as music, rituals, journaling, meditation, and so on.

The Relationship Between Content and Contemplative Practice

Faculty broke the agreement to privilege mental knowing described on pp. 26–32 in chapter 1 to create a pedagogic vision where personal reflection, insight, and emotion could coexist with intellectual learning. Figure 2 portrays three epistemological stances regarding the relationship between content and contemplation.

DUALISTIC. In the traditional dualistic stance, learning course content and engaging in deep personal reflection are usually perceived as two different processes that have little or nothing to do with each other. This is more the

Figure 2 Stances Reflecting the Relationship Between Content and Contemplation

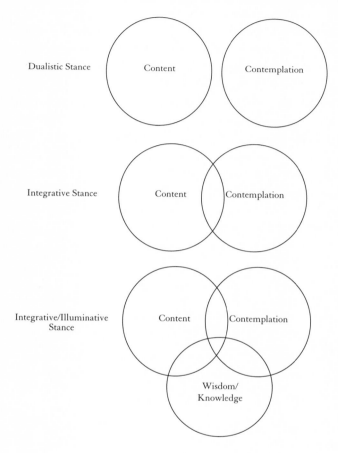

Dualistic Stance — Content — Contemplation

Integrative Stance — Content — Contemplation

Integrative/Illuminative Stance — Content — Contemplation — Wisdom/ Knowledge

epistemological rule than the exception in higher education, and faculty in this study did not embrace this kind of separation.

INTEGRATIVE. In the integrative view, content and contemplation are connected and complementary. In this chapter, I provided numerous examples of the use of contemplative practices designed to still the mind, allow for concentration and insight, and awaken the learner's connectedness to what was being learned. But here again, the idea is to see beyond the connection to ascertain what is taking place, as content and reflective practices are united.

INTEGRATIVE/ILLUMINATIVE. In Figure 2, I present a third stance, captured in the difrasismo Content.Contemplation.Wisdom/Knowledge. In the integrative/illuminative stance we also see the connection between content and contemplation, but the larger reality is that when the dualities are united, knowledge and wisdom may evolve. Wisdom can be associated with what Pulido called *"una persona educada,"* an educated person. What Pulido was alluding to is that a truly educated person is not simply one who has acquired great knowledge or who holds advanced degrees. *Una persona educada* is one graced with wisdom and able to apply knowledge with insight, intuitive awareness, and common sense.

Educación may be viewed as synonymous with wisdom, a complement to factual knowledge. Thompson and O'Dea (2001) write:

> Knowledge and wisdom are related yet different. Knowledge is the result of empirical observation and represents the consolidation of interpretations by observers of whatever is observed. It has been the hallmark of the Western scientific paradigm and has served a useful purpose. Wisdom is borne of personal and communal reflection on life as it unfolds; on happiness, suffering and the causes of each. It requires a maturing process which incorporates courage, insight, and, at times, letting go of the need to know and resting in paradox. Unlike knowledge, wisdom is rooted in much deeper psychological and spiritual soil. It requires the cultivation of multiple intelligences. (p. 6)

When faculty took time to create a reflective space to foster deep understanding, intuitive awareness, and fresh insights, wisdom became apparent in multiple ways. In Blake's class, key academic goals were for students to learn African American history, develop reading and writing skills, and become critical, reflective thinkers constantly engaged in learning. Through the use of contemplative practice, such as storytelling, photographs, and music, students were able to get closer to the subject matter and in the process learn African American history, as well as to gain wisdom in the form of developing self-awareness, acquiring a sense of purpose, and connecting their learning to personal experience. In the case of Cantú, she emphasized that students needed to develop their writing skills. However, she was able to turn writing into a contemplative practice tool by having students write about photographs that captured defining people and moments in their lives. Through this engaged learning experience, one student underwent an epiphanic moment learning more about her family and, in particular, her mother. The wisdom acquired here could be expressed as the ability to connect learning to personal experience and to recognize that knowledge and wisdom can begin from a personal space related to the student.

Pulido used cajitas as a contemplative practice activity in his Latino and ethnic studies courses. The cajitas turned students into what Pulido called a "community of artists" (2002, pp. 69–70), and his goal was not only to teach concepts such as cultural identity and religion that he needed to cover in class, but also to transform the lives of students in a way that they could apply knowledge in everyday life experiences. Connecting knowledge to everyday life can be considered a form of wisdom, for students begin to appreciate that knowledge does not exist in a vacuum. In the classroom when I taught research methods, I wanted my students to learn diverse qualitative and quantitative methodological approaches to conduct research. Also using cajitas, I helped students to acquire wisdom in the sense that they began to explore the deeper meaning of doing research, of how their studies were connected to their personal lives, and how their research was giving them a newly found sense of purpose and social responsibility. In Table 2, I distinguish the key differences between knowledge and wisdom.

In the integrative/illuminative stance, contemplative practices become tools to enhance meaning and to connect the learner to the learning experience. Pairing outer learning (intellectual understandings) with inner learning (reflective processes) can yield a broader form of education that generates factual knowledge of the course material, as well as deeper insights, which inform wisdom. A faculty member's key challenge is to find balance and harmony between inner and outer learning. A classroom that steers far from covering essential course content can be as diminished as one that does little or nothing to engage students in contemplative practice. Academic rigor should not be compromised. However, the goal is to foster the generation of academic knowledge and wisdom. In the next chapter, I describe how an integrative, consonant pedagogy can address issues of social justice.

Table 2 Recognizing Knowledge and Wisdom

Knowledge	Wisdom
Goal is to acquire facts and information	Goal is to develop self-awareness, sense of purpose
Focus is on learning, but not necessarily on applying knowledge	Focus is on learning and connecting information to everyday life
Based on rationality	Primarily based on intuition and feelings
Interpreted by detached observers	Arises from personal and communal reflection on life
Focus on outer experience	Focus on inner experience and self-reflexivity
Focus on learning for learning's sake	Focus on learning as well as social responsibility
Begins from "objective" space	Begins from personal space

4

Refashioning the Dream

THE EXPERIENCE OF EMPLOYING AN INTEGRATIVE, CONSONANT PEDAGOGY ROOTED IN SOCIAL JUSTICE

Compassion can be put into practice if one recognizes the fact that every human being is a member of humanity and the human family regardless of differences in religion, culture, color and creed. Deep down there is no difference.

—Dalai Lama

Often educators forget that one of the key aims of education is to be of service to the richly diverse human family. In education a key concern is how to foster in students a sense of compassion, social responsibility, ethics, and morality. When working with low-income students who have been marginalized, stereotyped, and invalidated, a key concern is to transform them into powerful learners able to recognize their strengths and able to view themselves as capable of consuming and creating knowledge. In Position I the aims of education could be expressed as follows: (a) to awaken inner wisdom and intellectual thought processes and (b) to promote self-reflexivity, which can lead to greater awareness and to connecting learners to the course material and to their inner wisdom. Achieving these two goals is significant, yet faculty in Position II went beyond these goals to emphasize activism, liberation, healing, and social change.

Position II: Employing an Integrative, Consonant Pedagogy Rooted in Social Justice

I provide two examples of faculty operating in Position II. The first is an English classroom in a community college where the professor works with low-income students, often the first in their family to attend college. The second is an art education classroom in a state university where the professor engages his students in social activism through the use of community service learning. While I highlight the experiences of only two faculty, it is important to note that social justice was a theme present in varying degrees in the classrooms of most other professors. To cite a few examples, Candace Kaye took her students to the Museum of Tolerance in Los Angeles. She said that during the visit they "were able to see the opposite of caring and the opposite of respecting humanity." To incorporate social responsibility, Norma Cantú engaged her students as literacy volunteers in the community. Susan Nummedal involved students in action projects, such as working in the university's multicultural center, to help them see that while social problems can be overwhelming, students do have some power to make a difference. J. Herman Blake's students participated in a multicultural learning community and in a national conference on race and ethnicity.

The Intersection of Integrative Pedagogy and Social Justice in an English Classroom

Social justice becomes a theme anytime faculty work with underserved students (i.e., low-income, first-generation, underrepresented) in a way that seeks to liberate them from past invalidating experiences that have fostered self-limiting views in order to transform them into powerful learners. An example of a classroom based on this kind of liberatory pedagogy is Barbara Jaffe's English class in California's Puente Project at El Camino College in Torrance, California. When I interviewed Jaffe, I also spoke to nine of her students who shared their experiences in the Puente English classroom.

Puente (Spanish for bridge) is a learning community that works primarily with low-income, first-generation Latino/Latina students, and a key goal is to help these students develop their academic skills so that they can transfer from the community college to a 4-year institution. Many of these students had been wounded by invalidating actions others had taken against them. For example, some had been told that they were incapable of doing college-level work, were treated as stupid or lazy, or were stereotyped. Working with Puente students is challenging yet exciting. It takes a special kind of professor and a unique kind of pedagogy to take these students from their self-doubts to a heightened awareness about their academic abilities and future potential.

The following outlines the elements of a pedagogy in which integrative, consonant teaching and learning meet social justice.

Liberating Students From Past Invalidation

Jaffe was aware that she needed to do everything she could to help students learn how to write and to develop as capable college students who could ultimately earn bachelor's degrees. She knew her class needed to have a strong academic focus— learning to write and developing study and time management skills. However, she did not stop there. She also knew that her students needed to be treated with kindness and compassion, and that she needed to facilitate their liberation from invalidating, self-limiting beliefs about their ability to succeed. One student related how a previous invalidating experience in her high school English class had cast doubts in her ability to learn. However, Jaffe's guidance and validating actions had appeared to liberate her to write and to express herself. Here is her story:

> In high school I used to have this English teacher. . . . There was a point when you turned in your assignment, and she would embarrass you with your writing. She would read the first introduction paragraph or your first topic sentence, and if it didn't really make sense or there was something wrong with that, she would read it out loud in front of the whole class and put you down and make you feel like your writing was not worth anything. . . . That's why I . . . had a fear of speaking out . . . whenever [Jaffe] would say you have to write something, I felt like, great, they [teachers] are going to put you down. They're going to say that my writing doesn't have any meaning. It doesn't make sense . . . [there are] grammatical errors. I wasn't going to be able to write a perfect paper. . . . The teachers in high school, they expect you to know something, but in a way they don't really teach you. And Barbara [Jaffe], she's gone through what needs to be in the introduction, what is the thesis statement. We've learned

a lot in this class. . . . I've noticed such a big change, and I am really thankful for being in the Puente program.

Jaffe understood that hers was no ordinary classroom. She knew that students who grew up in neighborhoods where hardly anyone has been to college and where students attended schools with limited resources were not likely to believe that they could be successful college students. Her class had students who had been invalidated in the past. Invalidation can be considered a form of oppression, a way that people in power exert dominance over others. In the educational arena, one way that oppression manifests itself is when teachers make their students feel doubtful about their ability to succeed.

To overcome past invalidation, the Puente classroom had an academic and interpersonal, validation-rich environment (Rendón, 2002) and was based on relationships. Students formed study groups, or *familias,* to write and to share their stories. Jaffe gave students her cell phone number, making herself accessible beyond the classroom. Students validated each other with support and encouragement. Jaffe also validated students by consistently communicating to them that they could write and be successful college students. Having the Puente program counselor in class with her was also instrumental in helping students sort through academic and personal issues. This kind of classroom context is not one that most underserved students are familiar with. One student said: "Some of us . . . at the beginning, we're in disbelief. We never get taught what we learned here." Another student pointed out that he had discovered that he was not by himself in the struggle to define himself as a competent college student. He said: "I found out I could write. You get a relationship with the Puente students, a friendship. You start building study groups. You call people on weekends or you just hang out."

Employing Writing as a Contemplative Practice Tool

Students needed to learn to write and express themselves, but they also needed to develop confidence and to find their self-worth and purpose in life. To meet these goals, Jaffe began to use writing as a contemplative practice tool. In her class, writing became a tool to connect students to the deeper aspects of themselves, their family, meaningful people in their lives, and their culture. In this fashion writing became a relational form of contemplative practice (Center for Contemplative Mind in Society, 2007). Students began to write not about something that was alien to them but about things that were close to their personal experiences. In this sense writing had a reflective element to it, allowing students to probe their inner wisdom; to liberate themselves from invalidating, self-limiting thoughts about their academic abilities; to find their voice; and to promote deeper self-awareness. When I asked Jaffe's students to describe the most powerful learning experience in their English class, one student said how writing about his name had inspired him to become more aware about his identity and the direction he was taking in life:

> I had to do a writing assignment and I had to write about myself. . . . I never thought any importance to my name. I just saw it as a name. The sound of it [pronounces his name]. No pizzazz. What's important about my name? I asked my mom, my family. I have a name that is shorter than most people. I kind of stand out. In my family I stand out, so I kind of have something similar as my name. That to me was powerful because I had to write that, and I was never asked to write about myself or my name. . . . And it really got my attention and it really made me look at myself. Who am I? What's my identity? And it's helped me accept who I am—a person, a student who's trying to learn and improve himself. [Who is trying to figure out], What direction am I going? Where do I want to go?

When Jaffe assessed a student's writing, she took care to be encouraging and supportive rather than punitive. She emphasized that the student was getting better at writing, that the topic selected was meaningful and important, and that the student should keep trying to improve his or her writing ability. This kind of gentle, compassionate guidance is perhaps what Richland College faculty meant when they spoke about "teaching with soft eyes," or constructing a classroom context imbued with encouragement, validation, and kindness.

Employing Participatory Epistemology

The English course was based on a participatory epistemology, which focused on the connection between the experiences of the students and the topics they studied in class. Accordingly, Jaffe's class was inclusive, reflecting the culture and affirming the voice of the student. She incorporated writings from Latino/Latina authors and brought Latino/Latina professionals to class to speak to students about their upbringing and how they succeeded in their profession. Writing assignments were centered on the personal experiences of the students, who were viewed not as people with vacuous minds but as competent learners who were capable of consuming and creating knowledge. This is a form of participatory epistemology that connects students to the learning experience, eliciting greater awareness about the subject matter and about themselves as learners and as human beings. One student said that being exposed to Hispanic writers and speakers was the most meaningful to her. "They made me feel I can do it too. [The content] doesn't keep us away from our own roots," she said.

Positioning the Faculty Member as a
Social Change Agent, Healer, and Liberator

Jaffe was clear that her role was not simply to teach English. A key aspect was having students believe in themselves and in their inherent capacity to learn. She became not only an English instructor, but also a social change agent, a healer and liberator with a commitment to transforming students into competent learners able to shape their own lives. She spoke about the importance of what she called *collateral learning*. When I asked her what she meant, she said:

> Well, there's the English part of the class, and I certainly hope that they take away stronger writing skills. But beyond that, it's what happens while I am teaching the English . . . and probably the most important element that I want students to take away is that they have a sense of accountability to themselves and [that they develop] responsibility. . . . Students can be totally successful when they don't see themselves as victims; when they see themselves as creators.

Jaffe was passionate about helping students see beyond their limitations, to view themselves as knowers and to know that the knowledge they brought to the classroom was as valid as any other. When I asked her about her teaching approach, she said:

> First of all, I believe anyone can learn. But not everyone can teach so people can learn. I feel that every student in my class is intelligent. Every student can earn an A. Every student is an A student, and I think it's up to me to allow them to see that, and sometimes their lightbulbs go on a bit later than some others, but I feel that is my calling, for more than just English, that [students] can see their own self-worth.

As such, Jaffe's role became extended to include social activism in the classroom. Her role was not only to teach students to write, but perhaps even more important, to help them to believe in themselves and in their inherent capacity to learn. The liberating effect of witnessing oneself as a competent learner, perhaps for the first time in a student's life, is quite powerful. One student articulated this sentiment by saying:

> What I want to say about being in Barbara's class . . . I just couldn't describe it in one word. When I first came the first semester, I didn't believe in myself. But through the first semester and the second . . . English is my second language. . . . I had a lot of concerns, a lot of doubts that if I am writing a paper, if it was going to be good or not, if it was going to make sense or not. The first time I wrote a paper, an essay for her, I loved the way she put, you can do it, just try, you write [well] and you've been improving. And all that is helping me to believe more in myself. . . . I have learned a lot, especially the academic part where I learned how to study, how to focus, and how to be motivated. But overall it's helped me to believe more in myself.

Construction of a New Pedagogical Dreamfield

Many educators do not believe students like those in the Puente Project can succeed, and most would rather work with academically strong students who have been privileged to attend well-funded, resource-rich schools. To work with low-income students, Jaffe understood she had to do something different. She had to break away from the tenets of the traditional pedagogical dream based on the following agreements that especially work against underserved students.

- Writing is a stand-alone activity disconnected from student lives.
- Only a few can learn and be successful college students.
- All that poor, first-generation students come to college with are deficits that are most likely insurmountable.
- The teacher's role is to be the expert detached from students.
- Putting down students is tough love that can result in real learning.
- English professors need not emphasize the culture of the students.
- The student's voice and whatever is personal is unimportant in the classroom.

In place of this old dream, Jaffe had created a new pedagogical model based on these new agreements that assisted underserved students to succeed:

- Writing can be employed as a contemplative practice tool, allowing students to express themselves and to reflect meaningfully on themes that are important to them.
- All can learn if given the tools and the opportunity to learn.
- Students from low-income backgrounds have strengths. They bring resilience, having overcome many difficult challenges in life. They bring their culture and their life experiences, which can be used as a base to foster learning.
- The teacher can and should engage in positive working relationships with students.
- Encouragement and validation are key to student learning and growth.
- Students can learn when exposed to an inclusive curriculum that takes into account their cultural perspectives.
- Students can develop self-confidence if given voice in the classroom.

The Intersection of Integrative, Consonant Pedagogy and Social Justice Emphasizing Community Service Learning

Carlos Silveira is an art professor at California State University, Long Beach, and employs a community service-learning component in his class as a means to connect students to social justice issues so that they can transform their values and become social activists and change agents. To create a service-based, activist pedagogy, Silveira was guided by the philosophy of his Brazilian counterpart, Paulo Freire (1971). Freire was an influential education philosopher who advocated that education should be framed around the lived experiences of students. He argued against the "banking model" of education where information was "deposited" into student minds, and believed that all human beings, given the proper tools, could deal critically with their own social and personal realities. Elements present in Silveira's pedagogical approach include the following.

Employing Community Service Learning
as Activist Contemplative Practice

Taking action and connecting theory to action was emphasized in Silveira's course, Cross-Cultural Perspectives in Art Education. He required students to do 15 hours of service learning with nonprofit organizations and social service agencies in Long Beach communities. For example, students worked with an organization called Being Alive, using art to help HIV-positive kids and families interact better at home. Students also worked with children from homeless families living in a shelter by providing art projects. His students worked with the Latino community to create a Day of the Dead event that featured altars, dancers, and storytellers. For Silveira, social justice work required an attitude and posture change, and these could be learned not only from books but also from direct experience. He recounted a particularly powerful memory of a student teacher he had placed at Oasis High School, a special high school in Long Beach for gay, lesbian, and transgender students who had been so harassed in the traditional school system that they had to be placed in a special educational facility. The student he placed at Oasis was "close to being a fundamentalist Christian," and after her first visit to the school, she returned to see Silveira, who said:

> She came to me completely appalled and said: "I cannot go there; this is against my views because the Bible says that homosexuality is wrong, and I just cannot go there." And I said: "No, you're going. You're going because you want to be a high school teacher. Probably 10 percent of your students

in high school will be gay, lesbian, bisexual, or transgendered. And if I notice that you have any problem discriminating against those kids, I will be the first one not to recommend you for student teaching. You have to develop this tolerance." She went and after the experience she came to me, crying. She gave me this beautiful card saying that she had learned a very important lesson in life about acceptance and tolerance. . . . She was going back and reevaluating her views as a Christian. . . . Those memories are very powerful for me. So basically, I will never be a burned-out professor.

In Silveira's case, he had the preparation, skills, competence, and philosophy, including trust from his students, to ask students to challenge themselves in this fashion. Clearly, not every professor can do what Silveira did with his students. In this case, the student appeared to trust Silveira in what he asked her to do, and that it would result in something helpful, if not transformative, for her. Indeed, that appears to be what happened.

Modeling Social Activism

Silveira is a model of a compassionate social change agent. He told me one of the most powerful teaching experiences for him was working with children who lived in *favelas,* very dangerous shantytowns in Brazil. The movie *City of God* (Meirelles, 2002) portrayed the violent nature of the favelas where children witnessed people being killed almost daily, the result of war between drug lords trying to control the favelas. Drug lords hired children as young as 9 years old as lookouts or soldiers. Many children did not grow up to reach their 20s. Silveira said that he wanted to give his country of birth what he had learned in the United States. Some educators might say that these poor children cannot learn and that they are unable to produce knowledge or to be critical thinkers. But Silveira would beg to differ. Employing the philosophy of Paulo Freire, he went to the favelas to use art as a tool to empower children, to turn them into critical thinkers able to use what Freire (1971) called a *critical consciousness* to become aware of their rights and responsibilities, to recognize problems they faced in their country and their communities, and to become change agents for a better society.

I could see the pride and satisfaction in Silveira's face when he showed me the photos of the children and the beautiful art they had created. In particular, I was impressed with the antiracist angel the children had made—half white, half brown—an angel to protect their communities. Each time he met with the children, he had them talk a bit about what they could do to make the favela a better community. He realized that, initially, these children had to be proud of their community and their history. Under his guidance, the children researched their history and asked their grandparents how the favela got started. He said the meetings turned out to be like group therapy because the kids began talking about their problems perhaps for the first time in their lives.

Employing Participatory Epistemology

Silveira employed a participatory epistemology, actively engaging students in art projects within their communities to foster student development and social change. Silveira engaged students in *working the community* through activist projects that extended beyond the classroom and into the social world of the community. The community became a base for taking student learning to a higher level. Activist practice served to awaken a critical consciousness (Freire, 1971) that enabled students to recognize social inequities and to take action to remediate them. In this sense, praxis (action, reflection, action) became an essential process for learning. This sophisticated level of engagement transcends what is typically known as *student involvement* (Astin, 1985): meeting with faculty on a consistent basis, taking advantage of services on campus, joining clubs and organizations, and so forth. Silveira employed community service as a pedagogy to connect his students with social issues in their communities. The objective was not only to engage students in learning but also to assist students in seeing hope and possibility and in becoming compassionate humanitarians.

Engaging Students in Self-Reflexivity

The process of working in the community included self-reflexivity designed to foster awareness and personal growth. Silveira spoke about how he evaluated students engaged in service learning:

In service learning we have a component that is very important, the reflection component, which can take place in several ways. For me it's a discussion [in the form of] a paper, a final paper, and weekly reflections. They have to reflect on the experience linking the theory in class with the experience in the community sites. But what they write or what they share in the classroom is not only on a cognitive level but affective. They have to tell me how they felt—how they feel about the experience, which is something that we forget sometimes. In the weekly reflections . . . I ask also for the emotional aspect.

In this fashion, self-reflexivity served to engage students in the examination of their values and beliefs and the emotions associated with them. Self-reflexivity became a sophisticated form of personal engagement that allowed students to note what was happening inside of them as they engaged in social justice work in communities.

Positioning the Faculty Member as a
Social Change Agent and Humanitarian

For Silveira, a professor's role went beyond teaching content and theory to include being a social change agent, humanitarian, and healer. Compassion and humanitarianism were essential to working with his students and for engaging in social justice activism. One of his role models was Mother Teresa. He appreciated her tough love and no-nonsense approach to social justice. When I asked Silveira what he wanted to see in his students, he said:

I think they have to first of all [be] humanitarians as teachers. They have to develop this sense of compassion that is extremely important in teaching. Of course the theory is extremely important in the classroom. . . . There is this beautiful story that [a woman] from India told me . . . about Mother Teresa. Her sister worked with Mother Teresa. The first day she was in an infirmary for people with leprosy. They were so disfigured that this woman—it was her first day—she went to Mother Teresa crying, she just couldn't take it. . . . [She said] I am supposed to feed them, but I don't know even where I should put the spoon. Mother Teresa turned to her and said, do you see a hole in their faces? And she says, yeah. So stick the food in it! So this says so much. . . . Yes, she was tough; she was very direct. . . . [But] it is not about me feeling terribly sad, it is not about me crying. It is about *doing something about it.*

Constructing a New Pedagogical Dreamfield

As I reflected on Silveira's vision for an education of humanitarianism and compassion, it became clear to me that he had broken several agreements that constitute the hegemony that exists in many art classrooms that employ a traditional pedagogy. These agreements include the following:

- Art is a thing of beauty with no connection to sociopolitical themes or to human healing.
- The curriculum is race, gender, and sexuality neutral.
- Real learning occurs only inside the classroom.
- Emotions are unimportant in pedagogical practice.
- A college professor's role is to be an academician confined to operate within the ivy walls of the academy.
- Poor students cannot learn.
- Real art is for elite galleries and museums.
- A professor's role is to keep a distance from students.

In place of this belief system, Silveira created a new pedagogical dream to create a borderless social justice classroom based on the following agreements:

- Art can transform, art has healing power. Art can be used to create sociopolitical awareness.
- Real learning occurs not just in the classroom but also in a field setting in a community where there is actual contact with people. This is where theory meets humanitarianism, compassion, and critical consciousness.
- The professor is not only a teacher but also a social activist—a change agent.

- Low-income students can learn when allowed to express their voice and to work on projects that reflect what they know and what they represent.
- Emotions and personal experiences are important elements in acquiring knowledge.
- The professor views students as colearners with mutual respect for each other.

Difrasismos Inherent in an Integrative, Consonant Pedagogy Rooted in Social Justice

As in Position I, the epistemological foundation that emerged in Position II focuses on

1. the relationship between the student and the subject matter (Object. Subject.Participatory Epistemology),
2. the relationship between content and contemplative practice (Content. Contemplation.Knowledge/Wisdom).

Faculty made a significant effort to foster the learner's deep engagement with the subject matter, creating a participatory epistemology based on integration and direct, subjective involvement.

Moreover, content and contemplative practice existed in a complementary role, not as separate and distinct concepts. Jaffe's English class was concerned not only with getting students to acquire good writing skills. Writing was also a tool to connect students to the deeper aspects of themselves and their culture. Silveira strove to teach students theory and knowledge behind art. Yet he was also concerned with having students recognize that art could be employed to create sociopolitical awareness. Jaffe and Silveira appeared to understand how connecting the subject matter with diverse forms of contemplative practice such as writing and community service learning could invite not simply the acquisition of skills and knowledge but, more important, the acquisition of wisdom. Jaffe employed writing as a contemplative practice tool, allowing students to write about topics with special meaning in their lives. In this fashion, students learned to write yet also acquired insightful wisdom in the form of connecting learning with personal experience, liberating themselves from self-limiting beliefs that they could not write or be competent college students, and finding their voice and self-worth. Silveira taught the theory and uses of art, but he also used community service as a contemplative, activist practice where students acquired wisdom in the form of developing critical consciousness, compassion, and self-awareness.

The Liberating, Socially Just Classroom

An analysis of Jaffe's and Silveira's pedagogic philosophy, positionality, and strategies reveals what could be defined as a liberating, socially just classroom, which includes the following features:

1. The pedagogic focus moves away from overprivileging competition, individual achievement, and self-interests, in order to move toward an emphasis on relationships and the betterment of the collective whole. Pitt (1998) has emphasized the need to challenge the dominant, corporate-oriented narrative about social justice, which focuses on the education of the individual for economic imperatives and self-interests. In this grand narrative it is perfectly acceptable to have the ends justify the means as long as the individual reaps benefits. Instead, Pitt advocates an education that emphasizes the betterment of community and that focuses on reciprocity and trust. The use of familias as collaborative writing groups and the emphasis on community service learning are examples of a pedagogy that centers the collective (as opposed to only the individual) in a pedagogy rooted in social justice.

2. Pedagogy promotes self-reflexivity and the emergence of a critically aware, socially responsible individual. The curriculum and learning activities promote skills for students to engage in political and social issues. Silveira's goal was to teach art and have students reevaluate and transform their values, to develop tolerance, to recognize social inequities and take action against them, and to examine their values, beliefs, and the emotions behind them.

3. The curriculum is democratic, inclusive, and reflective of student backgrounds and needs. Jaffe incorporated Latino/Latina authors and speakers in the classroom. Students were invited to write about what they

knew best—their families and their culture. Silveira placed his students in sites where social justice themes were highlighted, for example, a high school for gay and lesbian students and an organization that worked with HIV-positive children.

4. Teaching and learning strategies attend to the education of the whole person. Students develop their intellectual capacities, yet also develop themselves as human beings. The curriculum helps students build identity (i.e., understand themselves, recognize their path in life, and develop critical consciousness). Students are able to critically analyze dominant belief systems, recognize how others have imposed limiting beliefs on them, and liberate themselves from these negative views. Emotions are not excluded. In Silveira's classroom, assignments included a reflective component where students were asked about how they felt when they undertook service-learning activities. Similarly, Jaffe employed writing as a contemplative practice tool to connect students to their families and culture, an activity that often elicited heartfelt emotions.

5. The professor models social activism. Silveira modeled the behavior of working in a community for his students, traveling to Brazil to work in favelas with neglected children. Jaffe's work with low-income students in a special program is an example of an instructor concerned with equity and justice within the classroom context.

6. The professor promotes an ethic of care, compassion, and validation. Jaffe, who worked primarily with low-income, first-generation students in a community college, took care to validate students as capable of learning, worked with students with an ethic of care and compassion, and made herself accessible in and out of the classroom.

7. Teaching and learning fosters transformation in students. In Jaffe's English classroom, students began to define themselves as competent college students and to find their self-worth, sense of purpose, and voice. Silveira strove to assist students in becoming social change agents as well as caring, compassionate humanitarians.

8. The Western-based pedagogic model that overprivileges mental knowing, competition, monoculturalism, and separation is decentered. Instead,

the emphasis is on wholeness (i.e., intellectual, social, emotional, and spiritual development), community, inclusiveness, and relationships.

The Relationship Between Pedagogy and Social Justice

In Position II, I pose a third epistemological frame, which I capture in the difrasismo, Individual.Community.Social Justice. Figure 3 portrays the different ontological views about individuals and community. In the traditional, dualistic framework, the individual is construed to be separate from community. The *I* is not about the *we*. Individual achievement is prized over communal efforts; notions of merit and survival of the fittest may be said to apply here. Neither Jaffe nor Silveira adhered to a separatist, individualistic pedagogic framework. In the integrative framework, the *I* is about the *we*. The individual exists in relationship to the community. The terms *I* and *we* exist in complex stability. As Moodie (2004) notes, we must recognize the distinct consciousness of the individual human observer. However, this recognition should not neglect the total field the consciousness is part of.

The integrative/illuminative stance takes the integrative position a step further. If we focus our attention only on each individual term (individual, community) the gift inherent in the dualities becomes imperceptible. The difrasismo allows for the energy of our thoughts to take us beyond the dualities, allowing for breakthrough insights. The word *community* may be said to refer to the larger human family, while *individual* applies to a single person. When an individual acts responsibly to advance the collective, this can be interpreted as a form of social justice work. In Jaffe's case, she operated as an individual, as a compassionate humanitarian. But this role could only be accomplished in relationship with her students in the Puente learning community. She worked in relationship with oppressed students in a way that fostered their academic learning and released them from doubts about their ability to succeed. In the case of Silveira, he was an individual instructor who actively engaged his students in service learning as a way for students to connect to communities and become change agents. In this fashion, he was able to foster their critical consciousness and to engage students in the action, reflection, action process to become caring, responsible human beings.

Figure 3 Stances Reflecting the Relationship Between Individual and Community

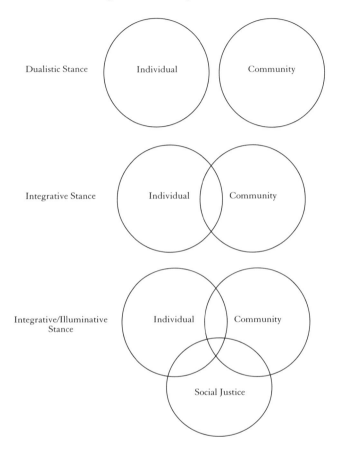

The reader should understand that it is entirely possible to work with an integrative, consonant pedagogy without a social justice focus. While some faculty in higher education do not view social justice as an area of interest for them, creating a pedagogy rooted in personal and social change interwoven with connectedness, caring, and compassion was a topic of interest for all faculty I interviewed.

Creating a new pedagogical Dreamfield based on wholeness, social justice, and liberation can be quite challenging. In the next chapter I elaborate on the experiences faculty had as they broke away from employing a traditional pedagogical framework. I also describe lessons learned from assessing students. Finally, I describe how students responded to their faculty and to the pedagogy they experienced.

5
The Courage to Chart a Different Path

If not now, when? If not me, who?
                                        —Hillel

Doing things differently in the face of resistance is an act of courage. At some point in their academic and personal journeys, certain faculty decided that it was time to break away from tradition, to think differently about what it took to teach, and to rethink their philosophy of assessing students. Students appeared to appreciate the effort of these faculty to follow their own path and to fashion a new pedagogic dream. In this chapter, I address key lessons learned from faculty who took risks and dared to break away from a stifling pedagogical vision that worked against wholeness. I also discuss the lessons learned from assessing students, as well as how students responded to their professors' pedagogic approaches and style of working with students.

Lessons on the Experience of Breaking Away From the Traditional Pedagogic Vision

The experience of breaking away from the traditional vision of teaching and learning was characterized by (a) recognizing the flaws of functioning in the old dream, (b) engaging in pedagogical and epistemological dissent, and (c) becoming confident with one's own style of teaching and learning. Tapping into their inner strength and commitment to remain authentic, faculty were able to shed at least some of the pieces of the entrenched teaching and learning vision based on rationality, disconnection, monoculturalism, and competition.

Recognizing the Flaws of the Old Vision

Unfortunately, most of us who teach are socialized to learn almost exclusively the traditions and conventions of an entrenched vision of teaching and learning. We start teaching with the limited tools we are given and with the framework we have been taught to adopt. As noted in chapter 1, the entrenched vision of teaching and learning is based on

- privileging intellectualism at the expense of inner knowing,
- disconnecting faculty from students,
- privileging competition over collaboration,
- leaving little room for error and imperfection,
- privileging Western structures of knowledge,
- engaging in busyness to the point of burnout, and
- discouraging self-reflexivity and time for renewal.

Most of us follow this model almost blindly partly because we have not been exposed to other models. Yet some of us begin to realize that the model is inadequate if not inappropriate. Psychology professor Nummedal explained how she has been socialized to be the all-knowing expert who could cover "boards and boards" of material:

> I lived in fear the entire first year that I wouldn't have ... enough material to cover in this allotted time because I had no way to gauge how rapidly this was going to go, and the other thing is that a student would ask a question. I was *terrified* that a student would actually ask a question because that meant, in my way of thinking, that I needed to know the answer, and I wasn't sure

I knew the answers to all these questions. So I made sure that I talked—very fast. I covered boards and boards and boards of material. . . . I felt really intimidated because there was a person teaching in the classroom before me who didn't always erase the boards. . . . I walked in and found that in this room not only were there boards in the front, but there were boards on the side, actually on three of the four sides. . . . She had covered the front board and the side boards completely and I only covered the front board! I mean it's embarrassing to think of what I did, but that's what I did; that's what I knew how to do.

Kristin Valentine described how her communications department privileged mental processes, as well as theory over practice.

[When] I arrived here in '76, I was told that 400-level courses should not be skills courses. You should not *do* in a classroom, you should only *think*. . . . What was being privileged in my department was social science. They were trying to be more scientific, I think, to give more credibility to communication. . . . I believe [that is where] they were headed. So, I was not only out there, because of the area that I taught, but I was told not to do any skills stuff, in other words [students] weren't supposed to stand up and read the poem. They were supposed to talk about how one studies performance but not do any of it. [But] I did it anyway!

Engaging in Pedagogical Dissent

To break away from entrenched structures inherent in the old vision of teaching and learning is an act of dissent and resistance. Intuitively, faculty knew there were flaws in the old model. While some faculty remained true to their philosophy of an integrative approach that honored inner and outer learning, some, for at least a short time, went along with the status quo, in part because they thought perhaps their vision of teaching and learning was not entirely correct. Over time, they learned to trust their internal logic, and their classroom became a place of resistance and liberation.

Nummedal explained the epiphanic moment when she was asked to work on a funded project to examine the development of reasoning in college students. It was during this time she realized that she would no longer be doing straight lecturing or paying attention only to cognitive skills:

> It was in that process that I made that shift and it was a pretty radical transformation. It didn't happen over a long period of time. . . . I very quickly began to engage students in discussions of things and invited them to work in groups. . . . I realized that what I knew was relevant, and that those [old] models that I had I could let go of. I used to get very nervous going into class. Wouldn't you be nervous if you thought the whole thing was your job? It used to make me incredibly anxious to go into class, and with that transformation I was able to realize, I'm prepared enough. What I need to do is be present in the room—pay attention to what's going on and to try to be a facilitator of what's happening, a good listener and a good responder and providing opportunities to do that as well. It became a very different kind of experience. It went from being nervous to being really excited because I never quite knew what was going to happen. But I wasn't worried about the right answer because I began to understand there weren't right answers. It was really liberating, it was very liberating. I mean there were answers, but they depend, and it wasn't for me to provide the right answer. That wasn't what the enterprise was about.

Pedagogical dissent involved designing overt and covert ways to work through the political structures of the institution. These include the following six methods:

Operating Under the Radar Screen

Valentine explained how she resisted the status quo in her communications department:

> I didn't tell the students I wasn't supposed to do it [employ a new pedagogy] because as soon as you tell them not to tell something, they'll tell. . . . So I just sort of did it, and waited to see if anybody noticed, but at the time they [her colleagues] weren't noticing what was going on in the classroom.

Nummedal explained her caution in letting others know how she approached her work:

> I try to be very careful in how I talk about what I'm doing because it is easy to have it dismissed, and I would find that somewhat painful for people to just say: Oh, you know that's Susan doing her thing. It doesn't really apply to what we are trying to do in the department. Until we as a department have deep conversations on student learning, I'm not comfortable giving a talk describing my work and how students in my classes learn and grow.

Emphasizing Scholarly Achievements

Intercultural education professor Li was aware that she might be viewed differently by her colleagues and adopted a strategy of developing herself as a formidable scholar. She said:

> I am writing research papers and going to national and international conferences to find, to get support, so that I don't get into trouble, especially [because] I'm not tenured. . . . I'm a good survivor and for me to do what I believe in is very, very important. And I am not saying I'm going to sacrifice my career. I'm saying from my philosophy and my believing Daoist philosophy I could always find my way. . . . I don't believe in either/or. I believe in both. I believe in inclusive philosophy, but I am highly aware of what might happen.

Similarly, early childhood education professor Kaye said that she published in "strong journals" and presented her research at competitive scholarly conferences, and that she understood she "needed to play the game." Education professor Crowell said he was not really comfortable playing institutional politics. However, he understood that for him to continue doing his own kind of pedagogy required an intellectual foundation, and that he had to have a very good reputation as a scholar in his field to legitimize what he was doing.

In Nummedal's case, she had been named a Carnegie Academy for the Scholarship of Teaching and Learning (CASTL) scholar, a prestigious award to work on diversity issues in a child development course. This award allowed her to engage in important work with the backing of the CASTL program. Even so, she said that one of her colleagues had cautioned her about being public with her work:

> I had the privilege of being supported through the Carnegie scholar program to do this work on diversity. And when I presented my project at a meeting at the end of the year, I got some feedback, which was interesting and at the same time very puzzling. . . . I talked about this work on diversity that we're doing together—my students and I. And, someone said, You know, I'm not sure you should go public with this. And one of the key things in the Carnegie work is that you make your teaching *public* so that others can build on it. And I thought, oh my gosh . . . this work is so important. We have to put it out there so that others can learn from it.

Adopting the Ethic of Working Harder Than Others

Valentine said:

> I was one of two women in the department, so I thought if I'm going to succeed here I've got to work harder than everybody else. I worked like hell, I served on every committee.

Finding Supportive Colleagues

Richland College faculty felt fortunate that they worked in an institution that supported holistic teaching and learning. Math professor Tinsley said:

> I'm really fortunate to be in a group [where] all of us go over math. We meet weekly and talk about how we improve things. . . . I feel pretty fortunate to be in a group where I can say what I think. That's a really important part of this place . . . that [there is] a sense of community not just in your area but across disciplines too.

Similarly, physical education professor Neal said:

It's always a nice cleansing opportunity for me to get away from the classroom for a day, enjoy the company of other people who I'm teaching with . . . enjoy some other people's perspectives on what they're doing in the classroom and how it's working for them.

Assuming Powerful Roles on Campus

Becoming a formidable figure on campus served to legitimize and shield some faculty from external criticism. Valentine said:

I became president of the Faculty of Women's Association. Now suddenly . . . we're talking the feminist revolution, talking the late '70s now, I'm president of the Faculty of Women's Association. Suddenly, I meet with the offices of provost [and] the vice president at that time every month, [and] I see the president of the university. I'm building this, you can't touch me. . . . So my strategy was to make myself invaluable to the department and the college and then untouchable because I had connections in high places.

Having a Strong Mentor

Ethnic studies professor Pulido spoke about how he had connected with a powerful faculty member on campus, "a quiet man" who operated "behind the scenes" and never took credit for what he did. His mentor was a senior professor who had the respect of many colleagues. This relationship appeared to protect him from academic threats related to his work. More importantly, Pulido now understood that he had to stand up for others who were trying to undertake similar risks because he had someone do that for him.

Becoming Confident With Their Own Style

Over time, most faculty had become adept at dealing with resistance and criticism from their colleagues. They knew they were being disobedient and defiant, but they were now more comfortable with their status and less troubled by what others said about them.

Acknowledging that there had to be a level of excellence, English professor Jaffe was aware that some faculty might think she was not being academic enough. But she appeared untroubled. She said:

First of all, I am not defensive at all. I think anyone can teach someone to write. A student can teach himself to write if they write enough and there's some feedback. But very few instructors address the issue of academics and the whole person.

When asked what she would tell her colleagues who might not be supportive of her teaching and learning methods, English professor Cantú said:

My first response is that yeah, OK, that's for you, and if you want to do your class like that, that's your class, that's the way you do it, that's your life, that's the way you've learned to do it, and I respect and honor it and I'm not going to try to change you. [But] it wouldn't work for me. And I could do it. I could march into a class, lecture for 40 minutes, give them a quiz every third class. I could do that, and it would be much easier to grade people that I don't know, that are just a number. It would be a lot easier to give a D to somebody I don't know, but when it's [a student] who had all kinds of problems at home. . . . It's harder for me than the other professors to give that grade.

Speaking almost defiantly, Valentine's response to unsupportive colleagues elicited the following:

What I would say to them now is, I am a full professor, I am director of the master's program, I've been president of the whole faculty. . . . I've been president of faculty of the Women's Association, and I've done all that [even] because of the way I teach.

Nummedal was comfortable with the fact that her teaching style might not work with every student and that not every professor ought to adopt her philosophy of teaching. She believes it is important for students to be exposed to more than her kind of pedagogy:

> I don't know that students need to have every one of their courses [taught this way]. . . . If they have a balance . . . a mix of things . . . it's a work in progress for me, but it seems to work with who I am and the kind of invitation I give my students to join the community for the period of time we have together. And they go from there to another kind of experience, and that's probably very healthy. They get to see a lot of different things. It's probably healthier than, well, I saw just one model.

When asked what she would say to traditionalists who might view her as soft on standards, Kaye responded in a very self-confident manner:

> I understand and I have been challenged by traditionalists. When I taught in the migrant program in San Antonio, Texas, I was told by the principal that I sat on the floor, and it was considered a negative because I needed to sit on the chair, I guess, for a position of power. But I sat on the floor with the children, and I stood up to that. I believe so strongly in this, and I believe there is a line of research and a line of study that shows that learning can occur in such an environment. . . . I also believe that the products that my students produce are strong enough. I have not been challenged by the "airy fairy" perceived notion of my style of teaching, although I know that some people will think that about my style. However, because it is so engrained in me, I cannot do it any other way because it is so authentic for my teaching self. And I have had enough success. . . . That's my baseline and I would stand up to it. I have agreed to be in a public university rather than a small private [one] where it would be a lot easier. . . . I believe this needs to be modeled as intellectual rigor within student centeredness and this needs to be shown in a public place, such as a public institution of higher learning. I don't want to say I'm militant about it. What would I say? I would stand up to them, with the understanding that I would not change their minds; that they would go away and they would still believe,

but I would still believe quite strongly. I have never had enough negativity to believe that I had to leave a position in higher education because of sharing power with students. And I will stay!

Similarly, Crowell pointed to his students as the best evidence that his pedagogical style produced highly competent individuals. "Look at my students!" he said. This sentiment was echoed by London who indicated he was pretty confident that his students could do as well as any other students on any kind of task.

Lessons on the Experience of Assessing Students

The human soul needs time to digest, absorb and comprehend emotions and experiences. Regardless of the external pressure or coercion, the soul cannot be rushed. We must metabolize events and feelings in order to fully apprehend them and understand our lives. It takes time for data to become wisdom.
—Wayne Muller

As Wayne Muller says, learning takes time; it cannot be rushed. In an educational culture obsessed with sorting and grading, it is obvious to me that we have lost touch with trusting the notion that learning is not bound by a specific timetable, and that all students can learn if given the right tools and proper guidance. Instead, we have created a culture where we evaluate not so much because we want to provide helpful feedback, but because we want to be absolutely sure that what we teach is being learned within the framework of an academic term.

In every interview, I asked faculty how they assessed students. This was a particularly important question because the goals these faculty set for students went beyond academic learning. I want to emphasize that faculty did not ignore academic rigor. They did employ traditional assessment tools, such as tests, quizzes, essays, and research papers. With these tools it was relatively easy to evaluate whether a student had mastered theories, facts, and figures. But the expectations these faculty had were remarkably high. They wanted students to master the course material, but they also said they wanted students to

- "See the glass as half full."
- "Have energy and enthusiasm and optimism for the world."

- "Make a difference in the world."
- "See that we are all connected."
- "Acknowledge themselves as human beings in this earth and to find their path, their passion."

Accordingly, the assessment philosophy that emerged was predicated on the following:

- Setting high standards and ensuring that students learned the course material
- Having trust and confidence that learning will continue, even as the semester ends, and that some forms of learning may never be able to be assessed within the confines of a specific semester
- Understanding the importance of providing constructive feedback
- Having trust and confidence in teaching methods to produce highly competent, reflective learners

It Is Important to Set High Standards for Learning

Often, educators believe that when a teacher begins to emphasize aspects of learning such as personal development and reflection, academic rigor is somehow compromised. I did not find this to be the case with the faculty I interviewed, and it is certainly not the case in my personal experience. All faculty spoke about the importance of having students learn the course material. In fact some of these professors believed their style of teaching promoted even higher standards than conventional approaches. Pulido talked about how he believed his standards were as high, if not higher, than those of his colleagues:

> I am not going to give a good grade to a student who can't write. They have to be able to write and to articulate themselves. I am not going to give credit to a student who can't read. I think if anything I would consider what I do is more challenging than what other folks are doing because you are having to look at things in very different way, and you are having to take the cannon of knowledge, whatever it is, and look at it very, very differently, and redefine it and mix it up and throw it around.

Blake shared with me how his assessment philosophy was as rigorous as traditional forms of assessment:

This one student who's working with me again this semester, she's a peer mentor, she said: "This is unlike any other course I've ever taken." I said, "Therefore you can't give me your traditional response." OK, that's what I do. Now is it assessment? I think so. Does it fit the assessment mode that a lot of people bring? I hope not! And, I don't apologize. I don't apologize because I think that what I bring to the students is very valuable, and hopefully it helps them to develop the capacity to *deal* with those other situations where others may . . . *expect* the traditional modes of assessment. Sometimes those traditional modes have serious detrimental consequences on a student's sense of self and I don't think I'm any less demanding, and perhaps [I'm] more demanding, and they come away knowing [they] can handle this stuff.

Education professor Crowell spoke about how he distinguished evaluation from assessment, and how students wrote and reflected in his class. When I asked him how he knew his students were learning what he wanted them to learn, he said:

I don't. I only know what they tell me. . . . I usually make a clear distinction at the beginning of every course between the essential question of evaluation and the essential question of assessment. In . . . evaluation you ask a question: Did you learn X, Y, or Z? What I wanted you to learn? Or what somebody wanted you to learn? And there are means of finding out whether or not they learned X, Y, or Z. But I think a more important question for me is the assessment question, which is: What did you learn? And I build that question in several reflective assignments. What did you learn that was significant for you? Can you explain its significance? Can you explore any revelations or insights that our activities in the course—the readings, the processes, the lectures, your work with others. . . . What happened as a result of this course to your thinking and learning? They are usually incredibly expressive. Sometimes I get they learned the content of the course. But more often than not . . . they are very expressive about transformations that took place.

Not that I try to identify what should take place. And sometimes those are quite surprising to me, what took place. They write about it, they reflect on it, they talk about it. Sometimes I will have them write a reflective essay at the end of the course, and they will share it then. Instead of a formal final exam, with four or five others they create a creative expression of what came out. And it is quite powerful sometimes, that level of insight.

Li emphasized that she did not exclude the learning of content or cognitive development. Rather, she tried to "keep the balance" between learning content and engaging in critical reflection.

Learning Takes Time and Continues Beyond the Academic Term

Overwhelmingly, faculty were more interested in the never-ending process of learning than of grading students, though grades were assigned. Intuitively, they understood that learning did not stop when the class ended, and that it might take a long time before a student internalized what was taught. Math education professor London said that some learning was difficult to measure and was "off the scale." In his view of assessment, some highly significant learning would not be able to be assessed immediately, and it might take a long-term study to capture the learning that took place over time.

Cantú elaborated on this point:

At the end of the class . . . I say, you may not think you learned anything, but I bet you did. . . . Not only that, 5 years from now, 10 years from now, 20 years from now . . . [when] you can say, Oh, I know that . . . and it's because of this class. . . . you won't even remember where you learned it, but that doesn't matter.

One particularly interesting assessment strategy was the use of postcards. Valentine, who taught communications, understood the temporal nature of learning. She was comfortable with the notion that the learning process would continue even after students had completed her course. One way she gauged this learning was through the use of postcards. She said:

> If you came to my door you would see postcards because I have always said to my students, when something happens anytime in your life that reminds you of this class or what we've talked about . . . because I'm pretty open about things that I'm interested in, just send me a postcard. A little post-card picture of something that reminded you and . . . I take them down every semester because I get my whole door covered with postcards. . . . I got a postcard from a former student who wrote from Vietnam who said, You said you could . . . sit down in any place in the world and learn some-thing about world traditions. I just learned what they do in terms of a fire dance and that reminded me of the class. So there's a connection, they've thought about me, and I remember them because in the classes that I teach they've performed for me, I never . . . I can't forget them. I don't just read their papers, but they *do* things.

African American studies professor Blake was adamant about the notion that students needed to be engaged in the constant process of thinking and reflecting. He understood that learning took place over time and in different ways for different students. He said:

> I know you look at people early and look at them late! But I don't know how you deal with the human process and turn it into a two-dimensional form. I mean, that's my problem! Fundamentally. How do you turn a process into a grade? Now a grade on a vegetable or vegetables helps you to sort. You figure out where they go. But you can't look at a student, you can't have a philosophy of learning and say there's no known limit and then say by 18 you must be at this point. . . . Well, some people don't reach that point until they're 28, others might reach it when they're 12.

Giving Students Constructive Feedback Is Important

In general, faculty felt confident that giving students valuable feedback was more important than grades. In fact, several did not believe in giving grades at all, but they assigned grades anyway because it was an expectation of the academy. Williams elaborates:

Tests are teaching tools, tests are not for punishment, tests are not for me to give you a grade; tests are for us to see where we are. . . . So that's real important to me. . . . for them to start focusing not on the grade but on, What have I learned? . . . How much have I learned?

Blake preferred not to give grades. He said:

I do not give grades, even though it *shocks* everybody. I give enough writing, and I believe an important part of learning is being able to articulate, and *writing* is a part of that. I give enough writing that I can see progress or lack of progress. I look at substance, not grammar or spelling. They have to write 13 essays and they get *progressively* more complex.

What Students Appreciated About Their Professors

Learning is about making your education very close to your personal experience or how you view yourself in terms of what's going on in society.
—Student in J. Herman Blake's African American Studies class

While I was able to interview only a small sample of students, the ones I did speak with provided some interesting perspectives regarding the pedagogy they had experienced. The following are examples of what students particularly appreciated about their instructors. I recognize the fact that future research should probe more deeply into the impact that an integrative pedagogy can have on students' intellectual, social, emotional, and spiritual development.

Holistic Approach to Teaching and Learning

Some students welcomed the blending of an intellectual and sensory approach. For example, one student who had taken Nummedal's psychology class said, "It was quite a relief to see a more humanistic and holistic approach being taken." A second student echoed this sentiment by saying, "To me, it's not just trying to engage students academically or intellectually, but to also engage them emotionally and to have students bring all of who they are [in the classroom]; who they are as a person and their lived experiences." One of Pulido's students indicated that pairing intellectualism with emotions was essential to student learning. He stressed that a holistic approach was "more powerful than anything you can read in the book. . . . I would argue, you need those kind of emotions, those kind of feelings because education is developing your mind . . . [and it is] also developing who you are."

The Professor as a Role Model, Mentor, and Friend

All students spoke about their professors in very favorable terms. It was evident that some students viewed their professors as more than just teachers or scholars. Some spoke about their professor as a mentor, and even a family figure. A student in Blake's class said she saw her professor as a father: "I would say, honestly . . . my relationship with him is somewhat . . . like a father-daughter relationship. I don't have a father . . . so like when I talk to him, it's not just academic; he knows me; he knows me personally."

One of Silviera's art students said that the instructor had become the example of the teacher she hoped she could ultimately become: "It made me see that: "*This* is the kind of teacher . . . I want to be!" Similarly, a student in Pulido's class said that as a result of what he had learned, he wanted to challenge the system. "I want to make my voice heard. I'm planning to be a teacher myself, a high school history teacher, and I also want to pass that on to younger students," he said.

One of Pulido's students talked about how he viewed his professor:

> I think that it's a relationship that has changed in the past couple of years. Initially it was . . . student-professor relationship, and then . . . sort of a mentor. . . . I think now it's at the point where I would say that, that we are friends, and that he has helped me a lot and that I know that if he had problems that . . . he could also share . . . with me. It's not, you know, a one-sided relationship; it is definitely reciprocal and . . . so I'd say that we are friends.

One of Nummedal's students also spoke of her instructor as a mentor:

> I've really appreciated her style, not just inside the classroom but outside the classroom, because her teaching style is a reflection of who she is to me.

And so outside the classroom, I've been able to ask her about a lot of different topics from my own personal struggles with going on to graduate school . . . and feeling supported in what I was doing.

The Professor's Investment in Students

The students did not want to disappoint or let down their professor because they felt he or she had invested so much in them. One student in Jaffe's English class summed it up this way: "I feel my spirit is alive. This keeps you alive. That's why you're here. You come back." Similarly, one of Blake's students said: "If I let [him] down, then that's just wrong, and so it just makes me want to work so much harder."

Students expressed great respect and admiration for the faculty, using words such as "patient," a "great person," "engaging," "nurturing," and "inspirational." One student in Bill Neal's physical education course summed up what students felt about their instructor: "There's not a single student in there that doesn't love him. . . . Students always like to pick on their professor, but not once have I even heard the slightest bit of criticism of Bill. Everybody who mentions his name, [they say] he's a neat guy, he's funny, he's entertaining, he's a great person."

Having a Validating Classroom Community

Students valued having a classroom based on community. A key element that students found very helpful was validation (Rendón, 1994). Examples of academic forms of validation came from students who said that their professors were challenging, didn't lower standards, provided meaningful feedback, and set high expectations of them. They valued professors who said positive things about their academic work and who pushed them beyond their perceived limits. One of Blake's students said:

> He can just simply tell you the difference in being . . . a student and a scholar. And then you can aspire to be a scholar rather than a student. A student is just being someone who takes information and repeats it. Being a scholar means you take information, you think, and that thinking shapes you in some way.

It is important, particularly for low-income, first-generation students of color, to be perceived as academically capable. The students I interviewed truly appreciated when faculty were able to see something more in them than what they were able to see in themselves. Interpersonal validation came about when faculty brought out the best of their students as human beings, recognized students by name, and affirmed them as individuals. One of Blake's students said, "The fact that he recognizes individuals or your presence, whether you are young, freshman, senior, graduate, or undergraduate, Black or White, he recognizes your presence. To me, that really validates me a lot."

Students also expressed appreciation for being in groups where relationships among students and faculty could be fostered. One of Pulido's students said:

> When you're in a group and you have . . . knowledge, you have education. You can kind of flourish from that and you can depend on yourself mostly, then you can depend on others, then you can depend on family, then you can depend on mentors, stuff like that to kind of *help* you . . . so you can move on and you can succeed and prosper, and you could do that and you could help others in the future.

One of Neal's physical education students expressed the importance of caring in her learning community:

> I said something one day about [the] end of exercise: "I can't believe you would have us hugging each other at the end of exercise when we're all so hot and sweaty." And he said, "You must understand that this is the only time some of these people ever get a hug."

Thinking Differently About Learning

A student in Professor Nummedal's class said that the material had "raised the bar of learning" for her, and had transformed what she believed about college-level learning.

> It helped me grow intellectually because the material was challenging. It did have me think about the material in a way that I hadn't previously been taught. . . . It wasn't just regurgitation. . . . I thought if this is what learning can be about—really engaging in the material and really feeling

like I had something to bring to the table . . . to me that, that set me in a new direction, and so that really facilitated my growth as a student and just overall person. . . . I had an opportunity to be in an environment where I thought, this is what learning should be. I want more of this, basically.

Another student commented:

I joined a study group and I hardly ever do that. It just I felt so comfortable with the other students in the class. . . . And in that class, which is one of the very few courses that I've ever joined a study group, there were several students in that class, and we were quite excited about studying for the exams because the exams were challenging. There was a lot that we knew that we had to try to look at in different ways. . . . Somebody else was going to see something that we didn't. Somebody else was going to hear something in a way that we didn't, and maybe that was going to help *us* put our pieces together. . . . It was a bonding experience.

Connecting a theory of transformation to student lives helped students in Pulido's class reflect more deeply about their personal transformation. One student said:

It was *definitely* beyond the scope of, you know, traditional knowledge and teaching. So, you really had to look at yourself and, and what was going on in your life. . . . [One of the foci] of the transformation theory is that once you come to some realization you can't go back.

Awakening a Social Consciousness and Personal Emancipation

The idea that education could be employed as a tool connected to personal transformation and social change in society was exciting and profoundly important for several students. Some students in Blake's African American studies classes remembered listening to the song "Strange Fruit" while viewing photos of individuals who had been lynched. The strange fruit referred to bodies of African American men hanged during a lynching. Students called this activity one of the most powerful experiences in class. One student said that it motivated him to become a humanitarian, to try to change the world. Another said, "It just hurt me and made me want to do something to better my life."

Other students in Blake's class became critically aware of how certain pieces of knowledge had been erased in their schooling. Students in Jaffe's English class were especially appreciative of having a curriculum that was inclusive of their culture, and stressed that reading Hispanic literature and having Latinos and Latinas speak in class validated their experience and made them feel that they too could be successful. One student said the curriculum "doesn't keep us away from our own roots." Similarly, Pulido's students expressed appreciation for learning Chicano history, which they had not previously been exposed to in other learning contexts. Because much of that history included examples of racism and discrimination, one student said that rather than not think about these issues and put them "on the back burner," he had now "learned how to face them and challenge them. . . . Then we become empowered." For this student, empowerment came through education, by learning how to "deal with White America or how to make yourself more accepted." Moreover, one student said she had learned that what she brought to the classroom was as valuable as any other student's experience.

Interestingly, when I asked faculty what they called the teaching and learning approach they were using, they had no term to describe it. In the next chapter I present a refashioned dream of teaching and learning that I call *Sentipensante Pedagogy*.

6

Sentipensante (Sensing/Thinking) Pedagogy

Why does one write, if not to put one's pieces together?
From the moment we enter school or church, education chops us into pieces: it teaches us to divorce soul from body and mind from heart.
The fishermen of the Colombian coast must be learned doctors of ethics and morality, for they invented the word, sentipensante, feeling-thinking, to define language that speaks the truth.

—Galeano, 1992

When I was searching for a term to identify the pedagogy that was emerging from my learning inquiry, a doctoral student directed me to a passage in Eduardo Galeano's (1989) *The Book of Embraces* containing the word *sentipensante,* which Galeano calls "Celebration of the Marriage of Heart and Mind" (p. 121). The word sentipensante comes from a combination of two Spanish words: *sentir,* which means to sense or feel, and *pensar,* to think. Galeano is taking the stance that rationality and intuition can exist in dynamic and complementary opposition. Our early ancestors all over the world recognized this epistemological position, but as consciousness evolved, Western philosophers assumed that intellectual training and rationality alone were key for understanding. Thomas Coburn (2005), president of Naropa University, recognizes two events in history that shape today's emphasis on the fragmented view of rationality and intuition:

When the Enlightenment set out to understand the external world in objective terms, apart from the inner life of the knower, it took a tack away from the holistic education that had previously characterized the Western academy and the classical traditions of learning throughout the Middle East and Asia, an education that aspired to nurture both the inner and the outer person. . . . The second recognition is that, ever since the Enlightenment, there has been a dialectic within the academy between two alternative ways of engaging with or construing the world." (p. 7)
—Excerpted with permission from *Liberal Education,* Summer/Fall, Copyright 2005 by the Association of American Colleges and Universities

Heinberg (1998) summarizes the views of Harman and Rheingold, explaining that that Descartes "launched the Western world on a belief system that, for the next three hundred years, would equate consciousness with thought. It is ironic, therefore, that Descartes' own radical new ideas were born in his own subconscious" (p. 125). Descartes' series of dreams and how they led to his insights about reforming human knowledge have been well documented through his biographers, such as Baillet (as cited in Gaukroger, 1997). Heinberg indicates that "many of our culture's most important achievements in the arts, science and technology were made by people who had breakthrough insights in dreams, visions, intuitive flashes, and altered states of consciousness" (p. 125). For example, Descartes analyzed his dreams, and Carl Jung worked with mandalas. Nonetheless, our modern culture remains obsessed with separating the workings of the mind from intuition, which is unexplained knowledge achieved through breakthrough insights, often occurring through contemplative means such as dreams, mandalas, and meditation, among others. To be sure, I credit many of the breakthroughs I experienced writing this book to periods of reflective practice.

In this chapter, I present a refashioned dream of teaching and learning, my vision of a model I call Sentipensante (sensing/thinking) Pedagogy, which represents a teaching and learning approach based on wholeness, harmony, social justice, and liberation. I develop the theoretical underpinnings and elements of Sentipensante Pedagogy from the lessons taken from my learning inquiry and from my own personal experiences in employing a sensing/thinking pedagogy.

Designing an Integrative, Consonant Pedagogy

For the purpose of this discussion, I define pedagogy as an approach that considers the professor's own philosophical orientation as well as the selection of appropriate teaching and learning strategies to set up an in- and out-of-class classroom context for learning to occur. I address the following 10 key questions that every instructor should consider in designing a pedagogy based on wholeness and consonance:

1. What is the epistemological foundation and what are the ontological assumptions underlying Sentipensante Pedagogy?
2. What are the goals of Sentipensante Pedagogy?
3. What are the strengths and limitations of a sensing/thinking pedagogical model?
4. Who is engaged and what are the forms of engagement?
5. What is the positionality of the instructor?
6. What is the focus of the curriculum?
7. What is the foundation of the classroom context?
8. How is a sensing/thinking pedagogy transformative and liberatory in nature?
9. What are the spiritual elements of Sentipensante Pedagogy?
10. What is the philosophy of assessment?

Epistemological Foundation and Ontological Assumptions

Perhaps the first step in moving toward a pedagogy based on integration and consonance is to recognize that the epistemology of wholeness and harmony is rooted in ancient wisdom. I am not now inventing the operant foundation for Sentipensante Pedagogy. Ancient epistemology is the first way of knowing, the way of our ancestors, the original way of the world. A number of scholars and philosophers such as Owen Barfield, Aldous Huxley, Miguel León-Portilla, and Roger Walsh, among others, expressed that our ancestors operated from a nondual state of mind. The nondual consciousness in the ancient world was dramatically different from our present ways of knowing. For example, the builders of the pyramids in Egypt, Tikal, Chichén Itzá, Tulum, Teotihuacán, as well as the creators of Stonehenge and the authors of the Maya council book, *Popul Vuh,* were demonstrably intelligent, yet it is likely that they did not think and learn as we presently do. Ancestral ways of knowing were based on wholeness. Ancient ways of knowing focused on the complementarity that exists between two opposites, resulting in a multiperspectival yet unitive view of the world. Faith and reason, as well as science and the divine, were not separate but viewed as two parts of one whole (Palmer, 1998).

As I explained in chapter 3 on pp. 67–68, a difrasismo is a stylistic concept in the Aztec culture where a pair of words is employed to refer to a third term or phrase. The third term reveals the hidden wisdom behind the paired dualities. In modern times we might consider a difrasismo as a dialectical space where two interacting themes exist in tension with one another. In a difrasismo, a larger truth emerges from illuminating the hidden mysteries of the paired realities, which dance interdependently and in grand cooperation with each other (Spilsbury & Bryner, 1992). In essence the difrasismo represents the resolution of dualities, the reconciliation of paradox.

In the introduction to this book, I explained that the term *integrative* is being used in at least two ways. In one view integrative learning connects skills and knowledge from diverse sources and experiences, as well as crosses disciplinary boundaries (American Association of Colleges and Universities & Carnegie Foundation for the Advancement of Teaching, 2004). The second view recognizes connections among diverse ways of knowing but also emphasizes the relationship between mind, body, and spirit, and the connection between the outer life of vocation and professional responsibility and the inner life of personal development, meaning, and purpose.

How does Sentipensante Pedagogy inform integrative learning? Sentipensante Pedagogy is integrative in the sense that it focuses on wholeness and nonduality. For example, it represents the reunification of sensing and thinking to foster the acquisition of knowledge and wisdom. The approach also partners the content to be studied with the learner to create a relationship that Owen Barfield (Lachman, 1998) termed *participatory epistemology.* In this epistemological stance, the learner is actively connected to what is being learned, and diverse forms of contemplative practice become conduits to elicit deep awareness, focus, compassion, social change, transformation, creativity, and inspiration, as well as intellectual understandings. Sentipensante Pedagogy acknowledges that two seemingly opposing concepts are actually two sides of a larger reality. A key ontological principle of Sentipensante Pedagogy is that it asks instructors to work with individuals as whole human beings—intellectual, social, emotional, and spiritual.

A sensing/thinking pedagogy is also transdisciplinary in nature. It is open to diverse disciplinary approaches to learning, and recognizes that learning can be enhanced with access to diverse forms of knowledge. This pedagogic approach recognizes the connection between Western and non-Western ways of knowing, the scientific method, and knowledge derived from the humanities and social sciences, as well as the spiritual experience. The pedagogy values intellectual understandings derived from scientific exploration yet is also open to the role of intuition, creativity, and imagination. Sentipensante Pedagogy values the individual's quest for knowledge yet also acknowledges the importance of dialogue and the shared construction of meaning. A sensing/thinking pedagogy also strives for balance and harmony; there is consonance between inner work, focusing on emotional and spiritual nurturance, and outer work, involving service and action in the world.

Goals

What does it mean to be truly educated in the world today? We are being challenged to educate students for a complex future with never-ending, ever more difficult social, political, and cultural challenges that test our ability to make sound, ethical, and moral decisions, as well as to make the world peaceful, equitable, and survivable. A sentipensante approach strives to foster the educated person of the 21st century. Accordingly, Sentipensante Pedagogy works with three goals. The first is to disrupt and transform the entrenched belief system, which is being held in mass consciousness, and its corresponding shared beliefs (agreements) about teaching and learning that act against wholeness and appreciation of truth in all forms. These agreements divorce the mind from the senses and separate the learner from what is being studied. The entrenched belief system privileges separation, monodisciplinarity, competition, intellectualism, and passivity at the expense of collaboration, transdisciplinarity, intuition, and active learning, especially that focused on social change. In our quest to transform the entrenched belief system, we must be willing to address questions such as: Why have I not broken out of a belief system that is oppressive in nature for many students and faculty? How is my behavior upholding power structures in the academy? What do I believe about who can and cannot learn? How am I choosing my curriculum—what assumptions do I follow, and is the curriculum truly inclusive and multicultural in nature? If not, what prevents me from doing this and why am I going along with this limiting view of knowledge?

A second goal is to cultivate *personas educadas,* well-rounded individuals who possess knowledge and wisdom. Personas educadas are able to work with facts, as well as with diverse forms of information and theoretical perspectives. Moreover, they are also able to apply knowledge with insight, intuitive awareness, and common sense. A third goal is to instill in learners a commitment to sustain life, maintain the rights of all people, and preserve nature and the harmony of our world. A sensing/thinking pedagogy is also concerned with eliciting social awareness within the student and teacher and some form of social change in and out of the classroom.

Strengths and Limitations

Sentipensante Pedagogy is not for every professor or for every student. A unitive, harmonious pedagogy is very challenging to prepare for and to implement. A significant amount of preparation is required from the instructor. Professors will need professional development in the uses of contemplative practice and the design of a relationship-centered classroom based on caring, trust, support, and validation. In addition, educators will need assistance with the development and incorporation of a curriculum that is inclusive of multicultural perspectives and worldviews and that is focused on social justice. A professor must be willing to take risks and to deal with emotions and tensions that often arise in class. Also important is the professor's openness and willingness to engage in self-reflexivity and in politically risky behavior to do things differently in the face of institutional resistance. In addition, professors need to be open to having more contact with students, as a sensing/thinking pedagogy will likely result in students' wanting to meet more often with the instructor.

Sentipensante Pedagogy is not for those who are uncomfortable with expressing emotions in class, do not wish to have extensive contact with students, are not open to collaboration and transdisciplinary learning, do not wish to employ strategies other than lectures, or are unwilling to share power with students in the classroom. It is best to avoid this type of pedagogy if it is not going to be employed carefully and if it is approached without enthusiasm. Nonetheless, in my experience the rewards of employing a sensing/thinking pedagogy can be significant. Professors will likely develop long-lasting relationships with students. Instructors may also be able to witness some form of transformation in their students (i.e., discovering self-worth, believing in themselves and their ability to learn, developing a critical consciousness, developing a sense of compassion, etc.). At its best, a sentipensante approach has the potential to create the kind of class that students will keep in their minds and hearts for a very long time.

Engagement

Sentipensante Pedagogy is concerned with engagement strategies that are associated with a rational and contemplative education. Accordingly, pedagogic strategies include traditional methods, such as reading and critically analyzing books, writing research papers, conducting experiments, writing critical essays, conducting lab work, and participating in class discussions. Contemplative activities are also employed, such as those described by the Center for Contemplative Mind in Society (2007) and discussed in chapter 2. These include stillness, movement, creation process, activist, generative, ritual/cyclical, and relational contemplative practices.

Two additional forms of engagement are particularly powerful. Engagement in social change can foster critical consciousness, which is the ability to challenge taken-for-granted beliefs, to critically analyze structural problems that preclude change, and to recognize social injustices and take action against them. Out-of-class learning can be particularly powerful in fostering critical consciousness, as students and faculty become involved in projects that seek to heal, transform, and liberate people who are suffering from social injustices. Introspection, or deep involvement in the critical examination of one's beliefs, assumptions, and worldviews, is a second form of engagement. Faculty and students must be willing to confront their own fears and biases and the extent of their participation in maintaining the status quo. Self-reflexivity can serve as a means for faculty and students to probe more deeply into what they are learning and how the learning is transforming them.

Figure 4 Faculty Positionality

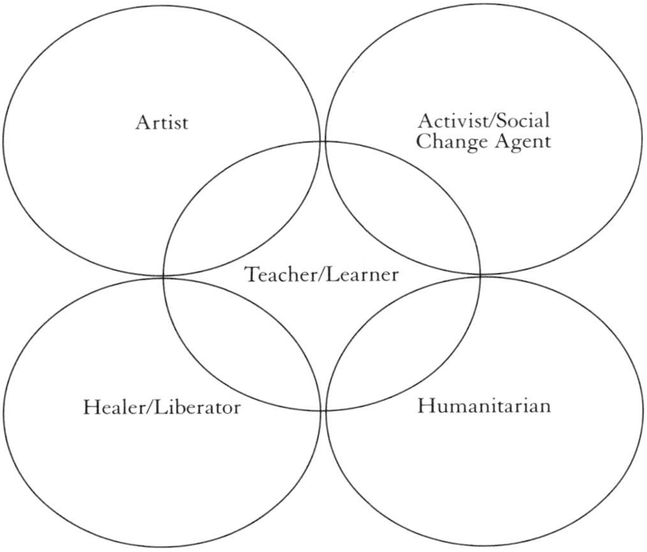

Faculty Positionality

Faculty positionality is portrayed in Figure 4. The instructor is conceptualized as (a) a teacher/learner, who possesses knowledge and expertise but who also realizes that no one human being knows everything, and that the key to learning is to remain open to the experience; (b) an artist, who fosters creativity and insightful thinking; (c) an activist/social agent, who is concerned with social justice work; (d) a healer/liberator, who can play a role in healing the wounds of students' past invalidation and releasing self-limiting beliefs; and (e) a humanitarian, who views teaching as a service to humanity.

Curricular Focus

With Sentipensante Pedagogy faculty are asked to create what I term a *multi-human* curriculum, meaning one that is multicultural and humanistic in nature.

This is an integrative, transdisciplinary pedagogy that affirms the dignity and worth of all people and respects and honors diverse ways of accessing truth (i.e., the traditional scientific paradigm, as well as the full range of qualitative methods that honor the human experience). A multihuman curriculum engages diverse perspectives, including feminist and masculine ways of knowing, ancestral teachings, and personal experiences, as well as Western, third world, and indigenous knowledges. Recognizing that content can often be biased, stereotypical, and exclusionary, a multihuman curriculum rejects one-sided perspectives and is inclusive in nature, respecting the fact that there are multiple ways to examine an issue, and recognizing that certain groups in society have been privileged in holding the keys to advancing knowledge. In essence a multihuman curriculum rejects a monocultural framework that Shiva (1993a) says is based on privileging a White race, a male gender, and Western perspectives. Content is carefully selected to weave in the contributions and perspectives of diverse groups.

A multihuman curriculum may be employed in and out of the classroom. Within the classroom, faculty may engage students in activities that promote broad, critical interpretations of who contributes to knowledge, how knowledge is defined, and the impact of such knowledge on worldviews, literature, history, legal systems, technology, economy, agriculture, architecture, and biological conservation, among others. For example, students might be involved in analyzing diverse interpretations of historical events and how these forms of knowledge have shaped our conceptions of democracy. A multihuman curriculum can employ community service learning as an activist form of contemplative practice. For instance, students and faculty could be involved in local, national, or international service-learning projects, which put them in touch with how diverse people view the world and nature, and how their knowledge has resulted in the creation of architectural styles, farming methods, and literature. As such, a multihuman curriculum invites critical, multicultural intellectual understandings, as well as promotes personal growth, humanitarianism, social change, and democratic processes. The possibilities of a multihuman curriculum are endless, requiring faculty to be open minded, creative, and willing to step outside the box to create a teaching and learning context that is multiperspectival and humanistic in nature.

Foundation of Classroom Context

Faculty who wish to employ a sentipensante approach need to set up the classroom for sensing/thinking processes to occur. In Sentipensante Pedagogy the classroom is based on relationships. Relationship-centered classrooms foster community, are caring and supportive, invite emotion, and find ways for students to bond, employing such strategies as engaging in group work and collaborative assignments. Moreover, these classrooms implement academic and interpersonal validation (Rendón, 1994) that affirm students as knowers and as valuable members of the learning community. Despite the emphasis on relationships and community building, faculty should recognize that attending to individuals is also important. Faculty can and should meet with students individually and provide one-on-one attention when necessary.

Transformative and Liberatory Aspects

Engaging Sentipensante Pedagogy can be transformative and liberatory. Every time faculty unlock the mystical truth behind polarities they are lifting the collective consciousness about teaching and learning and charting a new path toward wholeness. Every time faculty break entrenched agreements, such as giving primacy to the teacher, promoting passive learning, and privileging monocultural perspectives, they are working on transforming teaching and learning to create a new vision of education. In a new teaching and learning dream, pedagogic power is shared, learning is active, and teaching is centered in student lives. Student voice, feelings, and experience are welcomed, and multiculturalism and social action play a key role in learning. Learning academic concepts becomes as important as connecting with emotions and engaging in reflective processes.

The sensing/thinking approach I am outlining can also be considered liberatory in nature for faculty and for students. When faculty work with oppressed students while employing an ethic of care, compassion, and validation, they often liberate students from self-limiting views and help students find voice and self-worth. When faculty employ a multihuman canon, they liberate themselves from the myth of monoculturalism and the notion that humanistic, contemplative approaches cannot coexist with intellectual ways of knowing. Every time faculty resist and let go of entrenched structures based on fragmentation and one-sidedness to fashion a new pedagogy that is integrative and harmonic in nature, they liberate themselves and their students from institutional practices that work against their humanity. When students and faculty engage in projects that address inequality, discrimination, and oppression, they become social change agents who liberate others from social ills.

Spiritual Elements

The spiritual elements in Sentipensante Pedagogy include the use of diverse forms of contemplative practice, which may do two things: (a) quiet the mind to allow for the cultivation of deep insights and personal awareness, and (b) activate the senses as learners engage in social activism and self-transformation. Consequently, contemplative practice is two-dimensional. Contemplation may involve stillness and quieting the mind. Yet it may also involve stirring the soul, shaking up the learner's belief system, fostering a social justice consciousness, developing wisdom, and in the end transforming the self. Spirituality also manifests itself when caring, validating relationships are fostered among faculty and students, and when learning activities foster compassion, healing, creativity, humanitarianism, meaning, purpose, and awareness of the interconnectedness of life.

Philosophy of Assessment

With Sentipensante Pedagogy, the assessment philosophy is based on four key points. First, faculty can set high academic standards for learning and attend to goals related to personal growth, humanitarianism, and social change. Second, traditional assessment tools (i.e., tests, quizzes, research papers, etc.) can be employed and complemented by reflective assessment methods (i.e., journaling, student observations, group discussions, and reflective writing assignments, etc.). Third, tests and grades should not be used as punitive measures but as feedback mechanisms that assist in determining where the student is at a particular point in time. This feedback, offered consistently and constructively, can help guide learners to a higher level of evolution. Fourth is the acknowledgment that acquiring knowledge and wisdom takes time. Faculty are called to be comfortable with the notion that if they set up the right conditions some learning will occur in class, but additional learning may happen much later, even long after the semester ends.

Model of Sentipensante Pedagogy

Figure 5 portrays the model of Sentipensante Pedagogy. The model, guided by a nondual epistemology and ontology, is based on integration and consonance, representing the union of sensing and thinking processes and the balance between inner and outer knowing. The model includes six dialectical spaces expressed as a difrasismo where two concepts, critically examined to reveal how they differ and how they complement each other, illuminate a larger reality. In this fashion, intellectualism is united with intuition to reveal a holistic view of teaching and learning. Learners are engaged and connected with the subject matter to facilitate a participatory epistemology. Content is paired with diverse forms of contemplative practice to foster the acquisition of knowledge and wisdom.

In the model attention is placed on individuals as well as on the larger learning community. When individuals act responsibly to advance the collective, this may be considered a form of social justice. Individual faculty members can design a pedagogy that fosters a heightened critical awareness in students. For example, faculty can assist students to raise their self-awareness, find purpose, voice, and self-worth, as well as develop tolerance and learn to recognize social inequities and take action against them. Faculty can also help students to free themselves from negative beliefs imposed by others, to view themselves as capable learners who are able to consume and construct knowledge, and to become social change agents, as well as caring, compassionate humanitarians. Curricular materials are carefully chosen to reflect a multicultural and humanistic emphasis to create a multihuman curriculum that affirms diverse ways of knowing and the dignity and worth of all people. Assessment can be employed to gauge academic learning and to learn more about how students are maturing and moving forward with their personal growth (i.e., developing a sense of purpose, finding their path, discovering how they can make a difference in the

Figure 5 Model of Sentipensante (Sensing / Thinking) Pedagogy

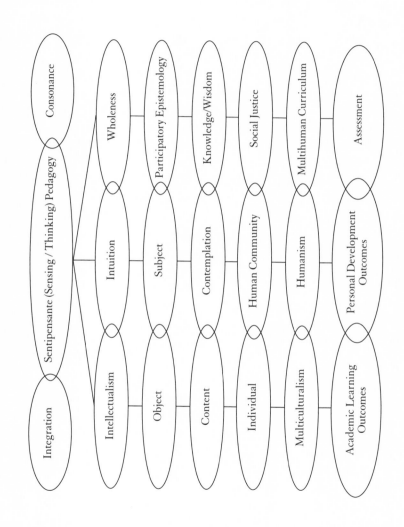

world, etc.). Some learning will continue over time and may not be able to be assessed within the confines of an academic term.

At the beginning of this book, I said that I am not alone on the path to create a new dream of teaching and learning in higher education. I issued a call for others to join me in the journey to transform institutional structures that work against our humanity. How do we sustain ourselves on this journey? The last chapter is intended to guide all who hear the call and who wish to embark on this path toward wholeness, social justice, and liberation.

7
Sustaining the Soul That Embraces a Different Truth

Turn loose the voices, undream the dreams.

—Galeano, 1992, p. 125

Having delivered presentations on the themes in this book to what must now be thousands of educators in the United States and beyond, I am usually asked questions such as:

- Should everyone respond to the call for transformation? How do we work with students and faculty who resist change and prefer to work within the status quo?
- How can you engage the work of transformation if you have no power in the institution? For example, if you are an assistant professor preparing for promotion and tenure, how do you work against entrenched, hegemonic institutional structures?
- How do faculty practice self-reflexivity and attend to self-renewal within a context that appears to privilege work addiction and to devalue time for self-development?

These important questions speak to the arduous reality of the contexts in which we work. Transforming our work and challenging hegemonic, institutional belief systems take a significant mental, physical, and emotional toll on those who find the courage to challenge traditions and to do things differently. What can sustain the soul that embraces a different truth?

Responding to the Call

This book calls on faculty to gather the courage to free their voices to articulate a different truth that speaks to creating a new pedagogical dream of teaching and learning. The calling is about revising the institutional belief system that works against wholeness and authenticity and to create empowering, holistic, multicultural, and participatory communities of learning. This is no small calling. Yet, the bell tolls unceasingly for educators who seek to connect inner and outer learning and to do things differently in the face of significant resistance. In his book *Callings: Finding and Following an Authentic Life,* Gregg Levoy (1997) says that responding to a calling requires knowing whether a call is really one we should respond to. Clearly, what I am advocating is not for everyone, and the kind of teaching and learning I propose should not be attempted by those who are not willing to carefully prepare to teach, to invest time and energy in self-reflexivity, and to take the risk of confronting dissent and resistance.

Perhaps the first step in discerning whether we should respond to the call is to consider two questions that Levoy (1997) proposes: "What is right for me?" and "Where am I willing to be led?" (p. 7). These questions involve a deep analysis regarding the extent to which we are willing to take risks. We must also be aware of the gifts we have to offer and how much we are willing to work on our professional and spiritual development to fill out our undeveloped talents and to know when and where to use them. Even more important is creating a life of passion, which involves embarking on a journey to fulfill a deeply desired goal. As Nepo (2000) said, "What makes you come alive can keep you alive, whether you are paid well for it or not. And beyond the fashion of the job market, a life of passion makes us a healthy cell in the body of the world" (p. 399).

Politics and Transformation

Most faculty that I interviewed had been teaching in their own way for a long time. Many did their work, often under the radar screen, telling nobody about how they taught. They were keenly aware of the dangers of making some of their work public. These dangers included not getting support for promotion and tenure, being viewed as troublemakers, and being perceived as touchy-feely or marginally intellectual. These are very real political issues that faculty must deal with as they engage in transformation.

I must confess that part of what sustains me in the academy is my hard-earned senior status as a faculty member. Even so, I have had my own struggles in bringing this work to the forefront of what is valued in higher education. Below are some strategies the faculty I interviewed identified that sustained them:

- being mentored by a powerful senior faculty member;
- becoming involved and assuming power in institutional governance, such as becoming president of the Faculty Senate;
- having a supportive community of like-minded faculty to turn to for sharing and collaboration;
- being a recipient of teaching awards that supported their endeavors;
- keeping an active research agenda (i.e., being perceived as scholars);
- operating under the radar screen and being cautious about whom to share their work with in their institution; and
- understanding that some faculty will never change and not worrying or even trying to do anything about it.

I emphasize that responding to a calling to employ a sentipensante approach carries significant responsibility. Just like any other pedagogical approach, the model I propose will not work for all faculty, and not all students will respond well to an approach that invokes heartfelt emotions as well as logical thought processes. Any new transformation is likely to involve us in shaking up a system while being shaken up ourselves. I also underscore that a sensing/thinking approach to teaching and learning is not always smooth, fun, and peaceful. While there are likely to be comforting and deeply rewarding aspects in invoking the mind and heart in the classroom, the stark reality is that tensions, conflicts, and chaos can and often do arise. One must be willing to work within the paradox that conflictual situations and chaotic disturbances are the guides to growth and true change. In releasing our voices and undreaming the dreams, we must be ready to face risk and be relatively comfortable in our vulnerability.

We should remember that there will always be those who resist change and who will try to manipulate circumstances to retain the status quo. Much resistance is based on fear, for all of us have invested much in the present status quo, and some rewards come from maintaining it. Yet fear prevents us not only from rising to a higher level of awareness but from seeing and experiencing our own authenticity. We must remain true to who we are and what we believe. How do we work with those who resist and trivialize our work? Perhaps one answer is to let go of outcome. We cannot control what others will do; we can only work on what we will do. We are not responsible for the actions of others, only our own. Perhaps others are not ready at this time to join the process of transformation. Perhaps they never will because their individual paths lead elsewhere.

The Courage to Transform: What Sustains Me

It is very easy to be overwhelmed when we attempt to do things differently. That is why so many of us give up when others become dismissive about our work or when we confront resistance or see continued social injustice. It is tempting to become frustrated and retreat to our shells that protect us from pain and harm. Yet, we must remain hopeful. One of the things that I have learned is that I may never see all the changes I want to see in my lifetime. However, I feel compelled to at least become part of the beginnings of change. What sustains me is knowing that I am not alone in creating change, and that many others are engaged in the struggle to create a new belief system and a new language that speaks the truth of who we are as human beings.

Perhaps my greatest strength is my past. For my past has given me my identity, the DNA of understanding social change from the eyes of a woman, a Latina who rose from poverty to better understand privilege in American society.

¿Quién soy yo? Who am I?
   The truth is that I am more than
   What I appear to be today.

¿Quién soy yo?
   No one really knows that I am
   The young girl who wanted nothing
   More than a pair of moccasins

For her sixth birthday
They seemed to be such
An extravagant purchase at the time.
It was a time when we lived
In a two room shack with an outhouse
It was the time that I had for so long
Cleverly blocked from my memory.
El dolor, the pain, numbs the senses.

¿Quién soy yo?
 I am the high school student
 Who didn't get invited to the senior prom
 Because she was unattractive,
 Unlike the girls who easily found their way
 Into school clubs and organizations
 Not for what they knew but for how
  they looked.
 The girl who was told by the sponsor
 Of the Future Teachers of America that
 She would never be a teacher because
 She had made an "F" in chemistry.
 "Teachers don't make F's," she said.
 She didn't know that I had sprained my knee
 So badly I could not walk to school for weeks.
 But there was no money to see the doctor
 Nomás no había dinero—this was
 just the way it was . . .

¿Quién soy yo?
 I am the graduate student who left Laredo
 To take the risks my parents were afraid of.
 The Chicana at the University of Michigan
 Filled with awe at the sheer fact
 That I was there, knowing full well
 Mi familia did not understand what I
 Was doing or where I was going . . .

¿Quién soy yo?
  Soy la mujer
  Haunted by my childhood memories
  Buried deep in my subconscious
  Appearing to me in dreams of evil spirits
  Wanting to penetrate
  Mi cuerpo
  Terrorizing my trembling body.

¿Quién soy yo?
  I am a multiplicity of identities
  That frighten me, guard me, teach me,
  Love me. (Rendón, 2000, pp. 10–11)

What sustains me today is the love I have in my life and knowing that I am not alone in seeking spiritual enlightenment and growth in all aspects of my personal and professional life. I am also sustained knowing that what I am doing is helping to make a positive difference in the lives of others. What sustains me is working on internalizing and practicing the teachings of my spiritual traditions. And I am sustained when I continue to work on becoming a gentler, wiser, humbler, and more loving person.

We can come to the space of enlightenment and spiritual strength in several ways, depending on the degree to which we are ready to work with what Palmer (2005) calls a "broken-open heart," one that is open to take in the largeness of life and to "hold one's own and the world's pain and joy" (p. 2). A heart that is broken open is humanly vulnerable yet spiritually strong. Heartbreak, while painful, can be the avenue for healing and developing compassion. How do we sustain ourselves when heartbreak seems ever present? Here are some examples of sustaining the soul that embraces a different truth:

- participating in a spiritual retreat individually or with others;
- adopting contemplative practices such as meditation, poetry, mandalas, art, music, tai chi, yoga, and so forth;
- engaging in social justice work that makes a significant difference in the lives of those in great need;
- taking care of our bodies through proper nourishment and exercise;

- making a pilgrimage to a place we hold sacred;
- forming a learning community with colleagues with similar interests;
- taking part in a learning, self-reflective experience, such as psychological therapy;
- taking quality time to be with loved ones;
- practicing forgiveness and compassion; and
- learning to say, "I love you," and meaning it.

In the beginning of this book, I invited you on a journey to create a new teaching and learning dream in higher education. By now I trust you have realized that the journey has its rewards as well as its discomforts. On the way to transforming education and to realizing a new pedagogical dream, our hearts are bound to be broken. Like Palmer, Nepo (2000) reminds us that all spiritual warriors must have a broken heart, because it is through those wide spaces that we can take in the wonders and mysteries of life. Nepo says:

> So what does it mean to be a spiritual warrior? It is far from being a soldier, but more the sincerity with which a soul faces itself in a daily way. It is the courage to be authentic that keeps us strong enough to withstand the heartbreak through which enlightenment can occur. And it is by honoring how life comes through us that we get the most out of living, not by keeping ourselves out of the way. The goal is to mix our hands in the earth, not to stay clean. (p. 56)

My hope in writing this book is that spiritual warriors who are on this magical journey to transform teaching and learning will not close their hearts in fear and pain. My hope is that we will not opt to remain always in sterile, lifeless, risk-averse spaces that shield us from getting the most of what it means to be alive. I sincerely hope that we will trust our intuitive sense, that oftentimes messiness, chaos, and heartbreak are ways the earth asks us to revel in its dirt so that cleansing may occur. My hope is that our hearts will remain open to see the world anew, to gather strength and courage to work only on those things that keep us present and alive.

To all those spiritual warriors embarking on this journey: Let us breathe through the cracks of our open hearts. And may our collective breath be the vision of a transformative dream of education that speaks the language of heart and mind and the truth of wholeness, harmony, social justice, and liberation.

Appendix

THE STORY OF MY INQUIRY

If we look back far enough in our own tradition, we can see that the word intellectual originally meant both heart and mind. . . . As the rational mind became dominant, the workings of the heart ceased to be intuitive but were considered irrational, and empiricists and romantics were pitted against each other, until those sharp with reasoning are now called cynical and those replete with feeling are now called sentimental.

—Nepo, 2000

What does it take to reclaim the integrative nature of heart and mind in a classroom setting? What are the elements of classrooms based on consonance, on honoring the harmonious rhythm between the outer world of action and service and the inner world of reflection, insight, and awareness? In an article I coauthored with Laura Burgis (Burgis & Rendón, 2006), we stated that intellectual pursuits are generally well understood (i.e., engaging in problem solving, decision making, and critical thinking). More difficult to understand is what it means to infuse heart into learning. Biologically speaking, the heart represents the center of the body, the seat of our very lives. We simply cannot live without a beating heart. Yet, there are other ways to think about the word *heart.* Palmer (2005) emphasizes that the heart can be thought of as the seat of human emotions and as the core of our sense of self. Metaphorically speaking, "learning with heart" could be seen as a process evoking human emotions and engaging learners in experiences that elicit a sense of wonder and appreciation for the sacred, as well as involving students in learning more about the self and how one is connected to a larger whole (hooks, 2003; Palmer, 1998; Rendón, 2005b; Shahjahan, 2005).

I wanted to conduct an unconventional study of college and university faculty who believed there had to be a better way for teaching and learning to occur in higher education, who understood, at least intuitively, that educating for heart was as important as fostering intellectual development. I wanted to learn from faculty who had found the courage to swim against the tide, who shattered the entrenched institutional belief system, and who worked within rigid institutional structures to pour heart and soul into teaching and learning. To arrive at a model of wholeness in higher education, I thought it would be important to conduct a study of faculty to learn firsthand about their journey toward reclaiming the integrative nature of teaching and learning and the pedagogical approaches they employed to foster intellectual, social, emotional, and spiritual forms of learning.

Methodological Approaches to My Learning Inquiry

My learning inquiry essentially blended conventional and unconventional research approaches. At one level, my inquiry employed what is known in the conventional research world as a *qualitative study,* where data come not from numbers but from narratives, which allows for the exploration of meanings, contexts, and images of reality. My research strategy specifically included multiple case studies (Yin, 1994) of unique college and university faculty ($n = 15$) who employed an integrative approach to teaching and learning. I provide a short bio of each faculty member in chapter 2. I tape-recorded all one-on-one interviews, and videotaped all but one faculty member. When possible, I also interviewed some of their students in focus group settings ($n = 23$), and I elaborate on faculty and student interviews in the last sections of this appendix.

But I did not wish to begin or end my inquiry with only traditional methods. A key issue in designing my learning inquiry was finding unconventional research methods to use in approaching my work. I sought methodological approaches that would allow me to (a) invite 2- and 4-year faculty to share their stories about what it takes to create a vision of teaching and learning based on the union between intellectualism and intuition; (b) position myself as a co-researcher with my informants and allow me to insert my personal experience into the research process itself; (c) employ, in every phase of the research process, methodological tools that could be considered spiritual in nature, such as meditation and creative expression; and (d) privilege the indigenous wisdom and engage in an anticolonial research approach. I wanted to work at the center and at the edge—engaging in epistemological extensions and modeling the blending of methods, perspectives, and discourses to push the envelope of what constitutes academic research and what is involved in uncovering truth. The key method I chose to employ was heuristic in nature, which I complemented with transpersonal research methods. Transpersonal methods (Braud & Anderson, 1998) and heuristic research (Moustakas, 1990) paved the way for me to engage as a coresearcher with the study's participants and to blend traditional approaches with creative, imaginative tools to explore the dynamic nature of a teaching and learning experience that transcends conventional practice.

Transpersonal Research

The methodology of transpersonal research grew out of the field of transpersonal psychology, whose epicenter is in northern California, and an early innovator was Abraham H. Maslow (1988). According to Anderson (1998)

> Transpersonal methods incorporate intuition, direct knowing, creative expression, alternative states of consciousness, dreamwork, storytelling, meditation, imagery, emotional and bodily cues, and other internal events *as possible strategies and procedures in all phases of research inquiry* [emphasis in original]. Both topics of research inquiry and methods employed are potentially transpersonal or spiritual in nature. Researchers, participants, and readers may be enlivened, even transformed, by the transpersonal elements of the study. (p. xxx)

While demanding and rigorous, transpersonal research can be imbued with wonder and joy. Transpersonal research approaches may be complemented by conventional qualitative and quantitative methods. Research can result in transformation in the investigator, especially when the researcher chooses a topic that is personally significant and heartfelt, allowing deeper engagement in the study. Likewise, opportunities exist for transformation and change in readers and participants involved in the study. Clinical application opportunities also exist, as transpersonal methods allow research participants to discuss personal issues, tell their stories, and generate new understandings and ways of knowing, doing, and being (Braud & Anderson, 1998).

Heuristic Research

Moustakas (1990) describes heuristic research as a

> process of internal search through which one discovers the nature and meaning of experience and develops methods and procedures for further investigation and analysis. The self of the researcher is present throughout the process and, while understanding the phenomenon with increasing depth, the researcher also experiences growing self-awareness and self-knowledge. Heuristic processes incorporate creative self-processes and self-discoveries. (p. 9)

As with phenomenology, heuristic inquiry involves understanding a phenomenon in human experience. However, heuristics puts equal emphasis on the people experiencing the phenomenon and on the researcher. It requires the researcher to have had the experience being explored. Moreover, the researcher should be attuned to self-awareness. The foregrounding of self-awareness may illuminate the intrigue and personal significance involved with the search to know.

According to Moustakas (1990) heuristic research involves six phases, which I paraphrase below.

1. INITIAL ENGAGEMENT. During this phase, the researcher is engaged in discovering a topic of intense interest, one that calls out to the researcher and holds important social and personal meaning. Moustakas says, "The initial engagement invites self-dialogue, an inner search to discover the topic and question. During this process one encounters the self, one's autobiography, and significant relationships within a social context. Ultimately, these forces come together and form a question. The question lingers within the researcher and awaits the disciplined commitment that will reveal its underlying meanings" (p. 27).

2. IMMERSION. Once a question has been identified, the researcher becomes immersed in the question in every aspect of everyday life. The researcher becomes keenly aware of everything that is connected with the question—social events, people, places, books, articles, dreams, and so on.

3. INCUBATION. In this process the researcher retreats from the intense concentration on the core question. Yet, the researcher knows that growth is taking place. The core question becomes the seed that is planted; the seed is given silent nourishment, and creative awareness results.

4 ILLUMINATION. As the researcher remains open to tacit knowledge and intuition, illumination occurs to reveal new elements of the experience. Corrections of distorted understandings or disclosure of hidden meanings may also occur through these awakenings.

5. EXPLICATION. In the explication process, the researcher pursues a full explanation of the descriptive qualities and themes that characterize the experience being investigated. New themes may be generated, and the researcher understands that internal frames of reference are needed, such as attending to self-awareness, feelings, thoughts, beliefs, and judgments. Focusing and indwelling allow the researcher to give concentrated attention to inner learnings and new discoveries.

6. CREATIVE SYNTHESIS. Having mastered knowledge of the material that elucidates and explicates the core question, the researcher moves toward the final process of putting findings and core themes into a creative synthesis. The synthesis is usually in narrative form, but may also be expressed in creative venues, such as poems, stories, drawings, and paintings.

Validation of data in heuristics research does not rely on statistical measurement. Moustakas (1990) explains:

> The question of validity is one of meaning: Does the ultimate depiction of the experience derived from one's own rigorous, exhausting self-searching and from the explications of others present comprehensively, vividly, and accurately the meanings and essences of the experience? This judgment is made by the primary researcher, who is the only person in the investigation who has undergone the heuristic inquiry from the beginning formulation of the question through the phases of incubation, illumination, explication, and creative synthesis not only with himself or herself, but with each and every co-researcher. (p. 32)

Consequently, verification of data involves the researcher returning again and again to raw data and even to research participants to share meanings and to check for comprehension and accuracy. After I completed chapters, which included the informants' stories, I communicated with all of my coresearchers. I asked them to review these chapters, specifically looking for the extent that the experience I articulated truly reflected their own. I also asked them to confirm that I could reveal their names and institutional affiliations. In the next section, I explain how I went through the processes involved in heuristic inquiry.

Living the Phases of Heuristic Research

As noted earlier, the first phase of heuristic inquiry begins with a core question, and Moustakas (1990) appeals to the scientist/artist to get inside the question and become one with it. The question had been burning in my soul for many years. I did not find the core question, the question found me.

Discovering the Core Question

When I applied for the Fetzer Institute Fellowship in 1998, I was literally feverish, sick with the flu, yet I knew my soul was healthy and I felt very alive with a passion to grow and to experience a profound awakening. At the time I did not fully understand how living a question could be agonizingly slow, confusing, and chaotic. I remember finding a passage from *Letters to a Young Poet* that German poet Rainer Maria Rilke (1996) wrote to a young man who was seemingly experiencing what Rilke called "a beautiful anxiety of life." In a narrative that often appears as a poetic expression, Rilke gently cautioned his younger colleague to

> have patience with everything unresolved in your heart and try to love the questions themselves as if they were locked in rooms or books written in a very foreign language. Don't search for the answers, which could not be given to you now, because you would not be able to live them. And the point is to live everything. Live the questions now. Perhaps then, someday far in the future, you will gradually, without even noticing it, live your way into the answer. (pp. 34–35)

This passage spoke to me over and over again during the time I was engaged in this study. My odyssey toward wholeness allowed me to develop a core question that would guide my inquiry into teaching and learning. This journey involved travel to learn more about my indigenous roots and to gain deeper insights into Latino spirituality in Mexico, Puerto Rico, Nicaragua, Guatemala, and Costa Rica. In these places I had the privilege of being a participant in experiences that tested my belief system about being an "expert" in education. A number of these experiences literally shook me up; it was as if I had stepped into a dark hole and had to learn to struggle to step into the light of greater awareness. In every location and with every event I took field notes, meditated on what I was learning, and wrote my reflections. My personal and professional life remain enriched through my experiences, such as attending a dream arts institute in the Yucatán, climbing the pyramids in Tikal and Teotihuacán, visiting a school for Quiché Maya children in a remote village in the highlands of Guatemala, and learning from spiritual healers in Costa Rica and Puerto Rico. I remain appreciative and humbled by the simplicity and power of what I learned and the impact of these teachings on me today.

I cannot say enough about how being a Fetzer Institute Fellow and attending retreats and seminars during three years opened the door for me to engage in this inquiry and to connect me to a deeper sense of who I am. I also presented my ideas to thousands of national and international educators through presentations at conferences, retreats, and workshops. During these times I engaged in conversations with faculty, administrators, and students that illuminated my thinking and verified the path I was taking. These opportunities to test my ideas also allowed me to refine and validate what I believe about teaching and learning. I also taught four graduate-level courses that covered topics such as student development theory, leadership and change, and research methods. In these courses, I incorporated contemplative practice activities such as journaling, mandalas, creative expressions, and meditation. My findings and conclusions are also guided by the truth of my experience as a teacher for 30 years in multiple settings, including middle school, community colleges, and 4-year colleges and universities.

Core Question

When I began to conceptualize my study about the relationship between mind and heart in the classroom, I knew I wanted this new work to be different from other kinds of research I had conducted. Intuitively, I sensed that I needed to explore the wisdom within me—all of my painful and joyous background experiences and the teachings of my ancestors had prepared me to be in this sacred place of exploration. Yet, I must admit that it was difficult, indeed frustrating, to come to terms with the notion that I could not do this work in the fast lane. It would take time, missed deadlines, incredible patience, and years before I put the pieces of my learning together, before I would be able to articulate the core question guiding my study:

> What is the experience of creating a teaching and learning dream (pedagogic vision) based on wholeness and consonance, respecting the harmonious rhythm between the outer experience of intellectualism and rational analysis and the inner dimension of insight, emotion, and awareness?

Immersing Myself in the Question

At the core of living the question is the paradox of the indivisible essence between self and others. To know others, I had to know myself. I realized that I had to experience what a unitive vision of mind and heart learning was and what it took to develop it. Moreover, if I was promoting an integrative model of teaching and learning for others, I had to live the experience of teaching with an integrative framework myself. In short, I had to walk my talk. I began to take risks with my graduate courses at California State University, Long Beach. When I taught Student Development Theory in Higher Education to a group of master's students, along with introducing theories of student development, I involved students in contemplative practice activities. I meditated before each class to determine how I could engage students more deeply in the material. During my meditative time, I discovered that I was not just teaching student development, I was teaching the answer to the question, Who am I? I wanted students to not only understand how college students developed their identity, I wanted them to get in tune with how they developed their own personal identification. To that end, I engaged students in periods of silence, journaling, and the construction of mandalas to reflect their identity.

When I taught Leadership and Change to graduate students at Iowa State University and to students in a joint doctoral program (University of California, Irvine, and California State University, Long Beach), I had students construct mandalas that reflected their own leadership style. Similarly, when I taught a course on research design for doctoral students, I had them construct research *cajitas* (sacred boxes), an activity I borrowed from one of my coresearchers, Alberto Pulido (2002), who had employed such an activity with his students in Latino and ethnic studies classes. I asked students to construct a *cajita* that reflected their research project—who or what had influenced their chosen topic, their ontological assumptions, and how their study might make a difference in the world of education. All of these activities were challenging to me as a teacher, for I did not know how my students would react, especially because these projects evoke intense emotion as students make connections between what could be articulated as the "black-and-white" theories they are learning and the "colors" of their personal experiences. Nonetheless, I was heartened because my student evaluations were quite positive, and students responded to me not just as a faculty member but also as a fellow human being.

Incubation

Many times I left my project because I became absorbed with other aspects of my professional life—new job, new responsibilities, different topics to study, and so forth. Yet, the study never left me. The study question was always in my mind and in my heart, and it appeared before me in different ways. For example, I was pleasantly surprised when a women's leadership team wanted to use my new agreements framework for developing new leadership models for women and people of color. Similarly, I was heartened when scholars interested in affirming diversity wanted to employ my new agreements model as a way to rethink institutional diversity work. I began to realize that my work could not only be applied to teaching and learning; it had implications for virtually everything higher education is engaged with—leadership, diversity, research, and service. I realized that while I might not be actively writing this book, everything else I was doing was related in some ways to my original intent.

Illumination

Throughout the multiyear research process, I tried to be aware of events and realities I might have missed or misunderstood. I reached greater awareness of my topic during the times I presented this work to national and international audiences. This gave me an opportunity not only to revisit my thinking but also to interact with others and, in the process, check how well my ideas resonated with higher education professionals. Writing this book was an intellectual and spiritual endeavor for me, for the book became a key outcome of my odyssey toward understanding and embracing wholeness and breaking away from old patterns such as self-avoidance and detachment. I read scientific articles and books on cognitive development and multiple intelligences, as well as books and articles related to science, religion, and philosophy. During quiet reflection, I often asked my ancestors for guidance. At times, I walked by the ocean and in the woods. At other times I listened to the snow as well as meditated privately when I wanted to break through an impasse or go deeper into a concept I could not fully understand. This was also an emotional process, at different times evoking tears, laughter, and/or prayer.

Explication

Chapters 3 through 6 are the key examples of my explication process, where I illuminate fundamental pedagogic positions and models that emerged from my learning inquiry. In chapter 3, rather than focus on each faculty member's teaching experience, I chose to present exemplary narratives, which generally spoke to the collective faculty experience. In chapter 4, I opted to present two exemplary portraits unique to each faculty member. The explication process was quite challenging, and I relied on transpersonal methods to assist me in focusing more deeply on the information that appeared before me. At times I found it helpful to pause and meditate when I was struggling with a particular theme. These pauses always resulted in greater clarity about what was emerging, and gave me direction in terms of how to articulate my findings.

Creative Synthesis

This book constitutes my creative synthesis. After living the experience of teaching for integration and consonance, giving myself time to reflect and to keep exploring my core question, sharing the findings that were emerging with national audiences, and sharing drafts of my writing with my coresearchers and colleagues, I felt ready to offer my work to the academy and to the world at large.

Interviewing Faculty

My learning inquiry employed a purposeful sample (Denzin & Lincoln, 2000) of 15 faculty in higher education (see Table 1 for the list of participants). The faculty included 10 instructors in 4-year and 5 in 2-year institutions. Of the 15 faculty, 7 were males, 10 were White, 3 were Latino/Latina, 1 was Asian, and 1 was African American. The key criterion I used to select faculty was that they had to have had experience employing holistic teaching and learning practices that included some form of contemplative practice in their courses (e.g., reflection periods, journaling, artistic expression, etc.). I also sought diversity in terms of gender, race/ethnicity, discipline, and institutional type (e.g., 2- and 4-year college faculty). I conducted one-on-one, semistructured interviews with faculty, which lasted between one and two hours. I began my learning inquiry interviewing four faculty at Richland College who were referred to me because they had participated in the Courage to Teach Program at the Fetzer Institute. This teacher renewal program designed by Parker Palmer (1998) is based on the premise that good teaching flows from the identity and integrity of the teacher. During my keynote addresses and workshops, I began sharing my preliminary thoughts about what I then termed *academics of the heart* (Rendón, 2000b). Invariably, individuals would come up to me to tell me about their colleagues who were doing similar work in the classroom. Using these references, as well as knowing which of my own colleagues were doing this kind of work, I subsequently identified 11 additional faculty to interview.

Following heuristic and transpersonal research methods, I positioned myself as a coresearcher with my interviewees, and I received my informants as partners and coresearchers who turned to one another in truth while we attempted to open the interhuman nature of the experience. Transpersonal research methods seek to extend conventional views of the qualities and role of the researcher. Braud and Anderson (1998) state that the researcher's qualities, sensitivities, and being are important "in all phases of the research project" (p. 20), because ultimately it is through the researcher's filters that all study materials are "collected, processed, interpreted, and expressed" (p. 21). This methodological perspective was important, as it allowed me to engage my own experiences and those of my coresearchers in my study.

Each faculty member received a formal invitation to be interviewed, including a copy of the interview protocol. Questions in the protocol related to issues that included what brought them to the teaching profession, their philosophy of teaching and learning, the most important things they wanted students to learn, assessment practices, the nature of their relationship with students, incorporation of diversity in courses, attending to individual and collective needs, powerful learning activities, use of contemplative practice activities, and obstacles to doing this kind of work. All except one coresearcher agreed to be videotaped. All gave me permission to reveal their name and institutional affiliation.

Interviewing Students

Because I wanted to get a sense of the influence these faculty had on students, I asked each faculty member to help me recruit students who had taken their classes and who would volunteer to be interviewed. However, only six faculty were able to recruit students because of scheduling problems. I interviewed 23 students (see Table A). These included 14 females, 13 Latinos/Latinas, 5 African Americans, and 5 White students. Each student received a formal invitation to be interviewed and a copy of the interview protocol. Students were asked if they would agree to be videotaped or tape-recorded and if I could have permission to release their names and institutional affiliation. One group of students declined to be videotaped, and they preferred that their names be kept confidential. The others gave me permission to use the tapes publicly. At their own choosing, in four instances, students were videotaped along with their instructor. I asked students to describe the kind of knowledge they had gained, how they characterized their relationship with faculty, the extent to which classroom materials reflected their backgrounds and individual needs, and the learning activities in which they gained the most insights about themselves as human beings. Lacking 100 percent permission to release names, I elected not to reveal any student name.

Table A Student Interview Participants

Faculty	Male	Female	Race/Ethnicity
Neal ($n = 2$)		2	White
Pulido ($n = 3$)	2	1	Latino/Latina
Blake ($n = 6$)	2	4	African American = 5, White = 1
Nummedal ($n = 2$)		2	White
Jaffe ($n = 9$)	5	4	Latino/Latina
Silveira ($n = 1$)		1	Latina

$N = 23$

Analysis of Transcripts

To analyze the data from my interviews, I worked with transcriptions as well as with videos of faculty and students. I was able to identify themes that emerged and articulate the story of the experience of creating a pedagogical vision that honored the integrative and consonant nature of teaching and learning. It is important to note here that transcripts and themes were reviewed not only in the traditional fashion. I also chose to receive the stories of my co-researchers through transpersonal methods, including a meditative process that facilitated the generation of new insights. Before reading each transcript, I meditated to seek deeper insights about what I was learning. This happened for each section of the learning inquiry and particularly when I got to chapters 3 and 4, as I attempted to capture the deeper meaning of the experience of teaching and learning for wholeness and harmony. At each impasse, I took a break to rest and meditate in order to facilitate breakthroughs in the conceptualization process. I also created mandalas and drawings that helped me to (a) understand my spiritual and intellectual role in writing this book and (b) frame and weave the threads of knowledge that were emerging. I paid attention to external cues that were going on in my life to think about what they might mean.

For validation and correction, I sent early drafts of two chapters to each co-researcher and asked them to provide commentary regarding the extent to which my analysis honored their experience. Further validation occurred when I presented my preliminary findings with educators at national and international conferences. These opportunities provided a forum for me to share my thinking and to interact with educators who provided feedback. At all times, I sought to honor the wisdom of my ancestors. I did this in two ways: (a) by reading and employing the philosophy of the Mayas and Aztecs and (b) through meditative states where I asked for guidance at each level of analysis. Rather than focus on every coresearcher as an individual, I chose to highlight representative faculty to tell the larger story about employing a sensing/thinking pedagogy. At numerous points I provide individual commentary to emphasize perspectives specific to each individual.

The use of video for interviewing and analyzing data is a relatively new approach, which has advantages and disadvantages. The advantages are that video makes visual and verbal and nonverbal behavior available for additional analysis, it is more effective than the print medium as a presentational method, and it provides a rich source of audio and visual data. However, some important considerations a researcher must address involve the issues of guaranteeing confidentiality and giving informants a choice on whether they wish to be videotaped or tape-recorded (especially in cases where informants are interviewed in groups). Other issues to consider include the possibility of the camera's presence creating feelings of intimidation and discomfort; the need to use high-quality, digital tapes to capture the best picture; the need for a high-quality digital camcorder; training in the use of video analysis and video editing; training in the use of video for research; and a room free of distractions and noise (Bauer & Gaskell, 2000; Loizos, 2000).

References

Abbott, D. (2000). Symbiosis. Retrieved June 17, 2008, from http://poliza.de/starship/sciencenew/symbiosis.htm

Albom, M. (1997). *Tuesdays with Morrie: An old man, a young man, and life's greatest lesson.* New York: Doubleday.

Allen, J. (Ed.). (2000). *Without sanctuary: Lynching photography in America.* Santa Fe, NM: Twin Palms.

American Association of Colleges and Universities (2007). Core commitments: Educating students for personal and social responsibility. Retrieved February 16, 2008, http://www.aacu.org/core_commitments

American Association of Colleges and Universities & Carnegie Foundation for the Advancement of Teaching. (2004). A statement on integrative learning. Retrieved February 16, 2008, http://www.aacu.org/integrative_learning/pdfs/ILP_Statement.pdf

Anderson, R. (1998). Intuitive inquiry: A transpersonal approach. In A. Braud & B. Anderson (Eds.), *Transpersonal research methods for the social sciences: Honoring the human experience* (pp. 69–94). Thousand Oaks, CA: Sage.

Arnheim, R. (1985). The double-edged mind: Intuition and the intellect. In Elliot Eisner (Ed.), *Learning and teaching the ways of knowing* (pp. 77–96). Chicago, IL: University of Chicago Press.

Arredondo, G. F., Hurtado, A., Klahn, N., Najera-Ramírez, O., & Zavella, P. (Eds.). (2003). *Chicana feminisms.* Durham, NC: Duke University Press.

Arrien, A. (1993). *The four-fold way: Walking the paths of the warrior, teacher, healer, and visionary.* San Francisco: Harper Collins.

Arrien, A. (1999). *The four-fold way: Teacher* (CD Recording). San Francisco: Harper Collins.

Astin, A. (1985). Involvement: The cornerstone for excellence. *Change, 17*(4), 35–39.

Astin, A. W., & Astin, H. S. (1999). *Meaning and spirituality in the lives of college faculty: A study of values, authenticity, and stress.* Los Angeles: University of California, Higher Education Institute.

Balam, C. (1989). The counsel of the Maya sage. In I. Nicholson (Ed.), *Mexican and Central American mythology* (p. 94). New York: Random House.

Barndt, D. (1989). *Naming the moment: Political analysis for action.* Toronto: Jesuit Center for Social Faith and Justice.

Bauer, M. W., & Gaskell, G. (Eds.). (2000). *Qualitative researching with text, image and sound.* Thousand Oaks, CA: Sage.

Belenky, M. F., Clinchy, B. M., Goldberger, N. R., & Tarule, J. M. (1986). *Women's ways of knowing.* New York: Basic Books.

Bernstein, R. (2007, May 17). *Minority population tops 100 million.* Retrieved February 29, 2008, from http://www.census.gov/Press-Release/ww/releases/archives/population/010048.html

Braud, A., & Anderson, B. (1998). *Transpersonal research methods for the social sciences: Honoring the human experience.* Thousand Oaks, CA: Sage.

Broomfield, J. (1997). *Other ways of knowing.* Rochester, VT: Inner Traditions International.

Bruneau, M.-F. (1998). *Women mystics confront the modern world.* New York: SUNY Press.

Buber, M. (1971). *I and thou* (W. Kaufman & S. G. Smith, Trans.), New York: Rockefeller. (Original work published 1923)

Burgis, L. M. (2000). *How learning communities foster intellectual, social, and spiritual growth.* Unpublished doctoral dissertation, Arizona State University, Tempe.

Burgis, L. M., & Rendón, L. I. (2006). Learning with heart and mind: Embracing wholeness in learning communities. *Religion and Education, 33*(2), 1–19.

Byron, G. G. (2005). *Don Juan.* New York: Penguin Group.

Cabrera, A. F., Crissman, J. L., Bernal, E. M., Nora, A., & Pascarella, E. T. (2002). Collaborative learning: Its impact on college students' development and diversity. *Journal of College Student Development, 43*(2), 20–34.

Cajete, G. A. (2000). *Native science.* Santa Fe, NM: Clear Light Publishers.

Cantú, N. (1997). *Canicula: Snapshots of a girlhood en la frontera.* Boston: Houghton Mifflin.

Cantú, N. (2001). Getting there cuando no hay camino. In Latina Feminist Group (Ed.), *Telling to live: Latina feminist testimonios* (p. 60). Duke, NC: Duke University Press.

Cantú, N. (2002). *Chicana traditions: Continuity and change.* Champaign: University of Illinois Press.

Carrette, J., & King, R. (2005). *Selling spirituality: The silent takeover of religion.* New York: Routledge.

Center for Contemplative Mind in Society. (2007). *What are contemplative practices?* Retrieved January 5, 2007, from http://www.contemplativemind.org/practices/index.html

Coburn, T. (2005, Fall). Secularism and spirituality in today's academy: A heuristic model. *Naropa Magazine,* pp. 7–8.

Cohen, A. (2000). *Embracing heaven and earth.* Lenox, MA: Moksha Press.

Collins, P. H. (2000). *Black feminist thought.* New York: Routledge.

Damasio, A. R. (1994). *Descartes' error.* New York: Avon Books.

Dei, G. J. S., Hall, B. L., & Rosenberg, D. G. (2000). *Indigenous knowledges in global contexts: Multiple readings of our world.* Toronto: University of Toronto Press.

Dei, G. J. S., & Kemph, A. (2006). *Anti-colonialism and education. The politics of resistance.* Rotterdam, The Netherlands: Sense Publishers.

Denzin, N. K., & Lincoln, Y. S. (2000). *Handbook of qualitative research.* Thousand Oaks, CA: Sage.

Derry, S. J., & Fischer, G. (2005, April). *Toward a model and theory for transdisciplinary graduate education.* Paper presented at the annual meeting of the American Educational Research Association, Montreal, Quebec, Canada. Retrieved February 16, 2008, http://l3d.cs.colorado.edu/~gerhard/papers/aera-montreal.pdf

Donnelly, J. (2002). Educating for a deeper sense of self. In J. P. Miller, & Y. Nakagawa (Eds.), *Nurturing our wholeness*. Brandon, VT: The Foundation for Educational Renewal.

Eck, D. L. (2001). *A new religious America: How a "Christian country" has now become the world's most religiously diverse nation*. San Francisco: Harper.

El Nasser, H., & Overberg, P. (2001). *USA Today* index charts rise in nation's diversity. Retrieved September 25, 2002, from http://www.usatoday.com/news/census/2001-03-14-diversityindex.htm

Ford-Grabowsky, M. (1995). *Prayers for all people*. New York: Doubleday.

Freire, P. (1971). *Pedagogy of the oppressed* (M. B. Ramos, Trans.). New York: Continuum.

Fuhrmann, B. S., & Grasha, A. F. (1983). The past, present, and future in college teaching: Where does your teaching fit? In B. S. Fuhrmann & A. F. Grasha (Eds.), *A practical handbook for college teachers* (pp. 5–19). New York: Little, Brown & Company.

Galeano, E. (1992). *The book of embraces*. New York: W. W. Norton.

García, M. (Ed.). (2000). *To teach with soft eyes: Reflections on the teacher/leaders formation experience*. Laguna Hills, CA: League for Innovation in the Community College.

Gardner, H. (1993a). *Multiple intelligences: The theory in practice*. New York: Basic Books.

Gardner, H. (1993b). *Frames of the mind: The theory of multiple intelligences*. New York: Basic Books.

Gardner, H. (1999). *Intelligence reframed: Multiple intelligences for the 21st century*. New York: Basic Books.

Gaukroger, S. (1995). *Descartes: An intellectual biography*. New York: Oxford University Press.

Gilligan, C. (1977). In a different voice: Women's conception of self and of morality. *Harvard Educational Review, 47*(4), 481–517.

Gilligan, C. (1982). *In a different voice*. Cambridge, MA: Harvard University Press.

Gladwell, M. (2000). *The tipping point*. New York: Little, Brown and Company.

Goleman, D. (1998). *Working with emotional intelligence*. New York: Bantam Books.

Goleman, D. (2003, February 4). Finding happiness: Cajole your brain to lean to the left. Retrieved June 27, 2008, from http://query.nytimes.com/gst/full page.html?res=9501E3DC1038F937A35751C0A9659C8B63&sec=&spon= &pagewanted=1

Goleman, D. (2005). *Emotional intelligence: Why it can matter more than IQ* (10th anniversary edition). New York: Bantam Books.

Goodsell-Love, A. (1999). What are learning communities? In J. H. Levin (Ed.), *Learning communities: New structures, new partnerships for learning* (Monograph No. 26, pp. 1–8). Columbia: University of South Carolina, National Resource Center for the First Year Experience and Students in Transition.

Gorski, P. (2000, Spring). Narrative of whiteness and multicultural education. *Electronic Magazine of Multicultural Education, 2*(1). Retrieved February 2, 2007, from http://www.eastern.edu/publications/emme/2000spring/gorski .html

Grande, S. (2004). *Red pedagogy.* New York: Rowman and Littlefield.

Greenspan, S. I. (1997). *The growth of the mind.* Reading, MA: Perseus Books.

Guerrero, M. A. (1996). Academic apartheid: American Indian studies and "multiculturalism." In A. F. Gordon & C. Newfield (Eds.), *Mapping multiculturalism* (pp. 49–63). Minneapolis: University of Minnesota Press.

Halifax, J. (1994). *The fruitful darkness.* San Francisco: Harper Collins.

Harding, S. (1991). *Whose science? Whose knowledge?* New York: Cornell University Press.

Heinberg, R. (1998). Lightning bolts and illuminations. In H. Palmer (Ed.), *Inner knowing: Consciousness, creativity, insight and intuition* (pp. 124–130). New York: J. P. Tarcher/Putnam.

hooks, b. (1994). *Teaching to transgress: Education as the practice of freedom.* New York: Routledge.

hooks, b. (2003). *Teaching community. A pedagogy of hope.* New York: Routledge.

Hurtado, A. (1996). *The color of privilege: Three blasphemies on race and feminism.* Ann Arbor: University of Michigan Press.

Institute of HeartMath Research Center. (2004). Science of the heart: Exploring the role of the heart in human performance. Retrieved June 29, 2004, from http://www.heartmath.org/research/science-of-theheart/soh_20.html

International Center for Transdisciplinary Studies and Research. (1994). Charter of transdisciplinarity. Retrieved February 16, 2008 from http://nicol.club.fr/ciret/english/charten.htm

Jay, K. (2001, October 12). Teaching as healing, at Ground Zero. *The Chronicle of Higher Education,* p. B20.

Lachman, G. (1998). The archaeology of consciousness: An interview with Owen Barfield. In H. Palmer (Ed.), *Inner Knowing: Consciousness, creativity, insight and intuition* (pp. 8–13). New York: J. P. Tarcher/Putnam.

Lardner, E. (2005). The heart of education: Translating diversity into equity. In E. Lardner & Associates (Eds.), *Diversity, educational equity and learning communities* (pp. 1–35). Learning Communities and Educational Reform, Summer. Olympia, WA: The Evergreen State College, Washington Center for Improving the Quality of Undergraduate Education.

Lather, P. (1991). *Getting smart: Feminist research and pedagogy with/in the postmodern.* New York: Routledge.

Latina Feminist Group. (2001). *Telling to live: Latina feminist testimonios.* Durham, NC: Duke University Press.

León-Portilla, M. (1963). *Aztec thought and culture: A study of ancient Nahuatl mind* (J. E. Davis, Trans.). Norman: University of Oklahoma Press. (Original work published 1963)

Levey, J., & Levey, M. (1998). *Living in balance: A dynamic approach for creating harmony and wholeness in a catholic world.* Berkeley, CA: Conari Press.

Levoy, G. (1997). *Callings: Finding and following an authentic life.* New York: Three Rivers Press.

Li, X. (2002). *Tao of life stories: Chinese language, poetry, and culture in education.* New York: Peter Lang.

Loizos, P. (2000). Video, film and photographs as research documents. In M. W. Bauer & G. Gaskell, *Qualitative research with text image and sound* (pp. 93–107). Thousand Oaks, CA: Sage

Lorde, A. (1984). *Sister outsider: Essays and speeches.* Berkeley, CA: Crossing Press.

Margulis, L. (1981). *Symbiosis in cell evolution.* San Francisco: W. H. Freeman.

Margulis, L. (2002). *Lynn Margulis: Scientific Guest of the Collegium Helveticum.* Retrieved January 24, 2007, from Collegium Helveticum http://www.collegium.ethz.ch/who/guests/index.en.html

Margulis, L., & Sagan, D. (1986). *Origins of sex*. New Haven, CT: Yale University Press.

Maslow, A. H. (1988). *Experiential knowing*. In H. Palmer (Ed.), *Inner Knowing: Consciousness, creativity, insight and intuition* (pp. 81–84). New York: J. P. Tarcher/Putnam.

Matthews, A. (2005). Mainstreaming transformative teaching. In P. Tripp & L. Muzzin (Eds.), *Teaching as activism*. McGill-Queen's University Press.

McGregor, S. L. T. (2004). The nature of transdisciplinary research and practice. Retrieved February 16, 2008, http://www.kon.org/hswp/archive/transdiscipl.pdf

Miller, M., & Taube, K. (1993). *The gods and symbols of ancient Mexico and the Maya*. New York: Thames and Hudson.

Miller, R. (1997). What *are schools for?: Holistic education in American culture*. Brandon, VT: Holistic Education.

Mitchell, S. (1998). *The essence of wisdom: Words from the masters to illuminate the spiritual path*. New York: Broadway Books.

Moodie, T. (2004, November). *Re-evaluating the idea of indigenous knowledge: Implications of anti-dualism in African philosophy and theology*. Paper presented at the 27th annual and international conference of the African Studies Association of Australia and the Pacific, University of Western Australia, Perth.

Moustakas, C. (1990). *Heuristic research: Design, methodology and applications*. London: Sage.

Muller, W. (1997). *How, then, shall we live?* New York: Bantam Books.

Muller, W. (1999). *Sabbath: Restoring the sacred rhythm of rest*. New York: Bantam Books.

Naropa University. (2008). Contemplative education. Retrieved February 25, 2008, http://www.naropa.edu/conted/index.cfm

Needleman, J. (2002). *The American soul: Restoring the wisdom of our founders*. New York: Penguin Group.

Nepo, M. (2000). *The book of awakening: Having the life you want by being present to the life you have*. Berkeley, CA: Conari Press.

Noddings, N. (1984). *Caring: A feminist approach to ethics and moral education*. Berkeley, CA: University of California Press.

Nussbaum, M. C. (2001). *Upheavals of though: The intelligence of emotions.* Cambridge, UK: Cambridge University Press.

Osei-Kofi, N., Richards, S., & Smith, D. (2004). Inclusion, reflection, and the politics of knowledge. In L. I. Rendón, M. Garcia, & D. Person (Eds.), *Transforming the first year of college for students of color* (Monograph No. 38, pp. 55–66). Columbia: University of South Carolina, National Resource Center for The First-Year Experience and Students in Transition.

Palmer, P. (1998). *The courage to teach: Exploring the inner landscape of a teacher's life.* San Francisco: Jossey-Bass.

Palmer, P. (2005). *The politics of the broken-hearted: Essay Number 8.* Kalamazoo, MI: The Fetzer Institute.

Pearsall, P. (1998). *The heart's code.* New York: Broadway Books.

Pitt, J. (1998, December). Social justice education in "new times." Paper delivered at the annual conference of the Australian Association for Research in Education, Coldstream, Victoria, Australia. Retrieved November 20, 2007, http://www.aare.edu.au/98pap/pit98177.htm

Principe, W. (1983). Toward defining spirituality. *Sciences Religieuses/Studies in Religion, 12,* 127–141.

Pulido, A. L. (2000). *The sacred world of the penitentes.* Washington, DC: Smithsonian Institution.

Pulido, A. L. (2002). The living color of students' lives: Bringing cajitas into the classroom. *Religion and Education, 29*(2), 69–77.

Quality Education for Minorities Project. (1990). *Education that works: An action plan for the education of minorities.* Cambridge, MA: Quality Education for Minorities Project.

Ramos, M. A., Ribeiro, A. B. (Producers), & Meirelles, F. (Director). (2002). *City of God* [Motion picture]. United States: Miramax Films.

Rendón, L. I. (1994). Validating culturally diverse students: Toward a new model of learning and student development. *Innovative Higher Education, 19*(1), 33–50.

Rendón, L. I. (2000a). Academics of the heart. *About Campus, 5*(3), 3–5.

Rendón, L. I. (2000b). Academics of the heart: Maintaining body, soul, and spirit. In M. Garcia (Ed.), *Succeeding in an academic career: A guide for faculty of color.* Westport, CT: Greenwood.

Rendón, L. I. (2000c). Academics of the heart: Reconnecting the scientific mind with the spirit's artistry. *The Review of Higher Education, 24*(1), 1–13.

Rendón, L. I. (2002). Community college Puente: A validating model of education. *Education Policy, 16*(4), 642–647.

Rendón, L. I. (2005a). Realizing a transformed pedagogical dreamfield: Recasting agreements for teaching and learning. *Spirituality in Education Newsletter, 2*(1).

Rendón, L. I. (2005b). Recasting agreements that govern teaching and learning: An intellectual and spiritual framework for transformation. *Religion and Education, 32*(1), 79–108.

Rendón, L. I., García, M., & Person, D. (Eds.). (2004). *Transforming the first year of college for students of color* (Monograph No. 38). Columbia: University of South Carolina, National Resource Center for The First-Year Experience and Students in Transition.

Rheingold, H., & Harman, L. (1998). *Higher creativity: Liberating the unconscious for breakthrough insights.* New York: J. P. Tarcher/Putnam.

Richland College. (2007). *ThunderValues.* Retrieved November 28, 2007, from http://www.rlc.dcccd.edu/thunderdoc/values.htm

Rilke, R. M. (1987). *Letters to a young poet* (S. Mitchell, Trans.). New York: Vintage Books. (Original work published 1908)

Ruiz, D. M. (1997). *The four agreements: A practical guide to personal freedom.* San Rafael, CA: Amber-Allen.

Sacks, P. (2000). *Standardized minds: The high price of America's testing culture and what we can do to change it.* Cambridge, MA: Perseus.

Shahjahan, R. A. (2005, November-December). Spirituality in the academy: Reclaiming from the margins and evoking a transformative way of knowing the world. *International Journal of Qualitative Studies in Education, 18*(6), 685–711.

Shahjahan, R. A. (2007). *The every day as sacred: Trailing back by the spiritual proof fence in the academy.* Unpublished doctoral dissertation, Ontario Institute for Studies in Education, University of Toronto, Ontario, Canada.

Shiva, V. (1993a). Understanding threats to biological and cultural diversity. Hopper Lecture, University of Guelph, Ontario, Canada. Retrieved February 5, 2007, from http://www.uoguelph.caresearch/international/documents/pdf/shiva1993.pdf

Shiva, V. (1993b). *Monocultures of the mind.* New York: Palgrave Macmillan.

Spilsbury, A., & Bryner, M. (1992). *The Mayan oracle.* Santa Fe, NM: Bear and Company.

Tarnas, R. (1998). The passion of the western mind. In H. Paler (Ed.), *Inner knowing: Consciousness, creativity, insight, and intuition* (pp. 14–20). New York: J. P. Tarcher/Putnam.

Tedlock, D. (1996). *Popol Vuh. The Mayan book of the dawn of life.* New York: Simon and Schuster.

Thompson, J., & O'Dea, J. (2001). *The spirit of human rights: Dialogues.* Kalamazoo, MI: Fetzer Institute.

Tuhiwai-Smith, L. (1999). *Decolonizing methodologies.* New York: Zed Books, Ltd.

United States Census Bureau. (2008). U.S. Hispanic population surpasses 45 million: Now 15 percent of total. Retrieved May 15, 2008, http://www.census .gov/Press-Release/www/releases/archives/population/011910.html

United States Code. (2008). *Oppressive child labor* [U.S. code title 29, chapter 8, § 203]. Retrieved June 26, 2008, from http://www.gpoaccess.gov/USCODE/ index.htm

Valenzuela, A. (1999). *Subtractive schooling: U.S.-Mexican youth and the politics of caring.* Albany, NY: SUNY Press.

Walsh, R. (1998). Hidden wisdom. In H. Palmer (Ed.), *Inner knowing: Consciousness, creativity, insight, and intuition* (pp. 21–23). New York: J. P. Tarcher/ Putnam.

Wolman, R. N. (2001). *Thinking with your soul.* New York: Harmony Books.

Yin, R. K. (1994). *Case study research: Design and method.* Thousand Oaks, CA: Sage.

Zohar, D., & Marshall, I. (2000). *SQ: Spiritual intelligence, the ultimate intelligence.* New York: Bloomsbury.

Permissions

Page 34

Palmer, P. (1998). *The Courage to Teach: Exploring the Inner Landscape of a Teacher's Life*. Reprinted with permission from John Wiley & Sons, Inc.

Pages 39–40

Cohen, A. Reprinted from *Embracing Heaven and Earth*. Copyright 2000, EnlightenNext, Inc. All rights reserved. www.enlightennext.org

Page 41

Shiva, V. *Monocultures of the Mind*. Copyright 1993. Reprinted with permission of Palgrave Macmillan.

Page 42

Tuhiwai Smith, L. *Decolonizing Methodologies*. Copyright 1999. Reprinted with permission of Zed Books, Ltd.

Page 43

P. H. Collins, *Black Feminist Thought: Knowledge, Consciousness and the Politics of Empowerment*. Copyright 2000. Routledge Publishing Inc. Reprinted with permission.

Page 56

Excerpted from *The Book of Awakening: Having the Life You Want by Being Present to the Life You Have* by Mark Nepo with permission from Conari

Press, imprint of Red Wheel/Weiser. www.redwheelweise.com Copyright 2000.

Page 70

Center for the Contemplative Mind in Society. *What are contemplative practices?* Copyright 2007. Permission granted by the Center for the Contemplative Mind in Society.

Page 131

Celebration of the Marriage of Heart and Mind, from *The Book of Embraces* by Eduardo Galeano, translated by Cedric Belfrage with Mark Schafer. Copyright 1989 by Eduardo Galeano. English translation copyright by Cedric Belfrage. Used by permission of the author and W.W. Norton & Company, Inc.

Pages 148–150

Rendón, L. I. (2000). "*¿Quién soy yo?* Who am I?" From *Succeeding in an Academic Career: A Guide for Faculty of Color*, edited by Mildred Garcia, Copyright 2000 by Mildred Garcia. Reproduced with permission of Grenwood Publishing Group, Inc., Westport, CT.

Page 156

Moustakas, C. *Heuristic Research: Design, Methodology and Applications*. Copyright 1990. Reprinted with permission from Sage Publications, Inc.

Index